€2-00

GW00835854

THE
EVANGELICAL
LIBRARY

The World Conquered by the Faithful Christian

by

Rev. Richard Alleine

"For whatsoever is born of God overcometh the world: and this is the victory that overcometh the world, even our faith." 1 John 5:4

Soli Deo Gloria Publications
...for instruction in righteousness...

Soli Deo Gloria Publications
P.O. Box 451, Morgan, PA 15064
(412) 221-1901/FAX 221-1902

*

The World Conquered by the Faithful Christian was first
published in 1668 and reprinted in 1834. This
Soli Deo Gloria reprint, in which spelling,
grammar, and formatting changes have
been made, is © 1995 by Don Kistler
and Soli Deo Gloria.

*

ISBN 1-57358-018-X

Contents

The World Conquered

Introduction

There is a twofold description given of the true Christian by the Apostle John, "Whosoever believeth that Jesus is the Christ is born of God," and again, "Whatsoever is born of God overcometh the world, even our faith," 1 John 5:1,4.

A true Christian, then, is a conqueror, more heroic, more noble, more exalted than the greatest of all earthly conquerors, for he has conquered that which has conquered them—the world.

Now, what is the nature of this victory? This, dear friends, is a very important question. We reply that it is a spiritual victory which can only be obtained by faith. "This is the victory that overcometh the world, even our faith."

The world is thus described by the Apostle: "For all that is in the world, the lust of the flesh, and the lust of the eyes, and the pride of life, is not of the Father, but is of the world," 1 John 2:16.

Faith is that living principle by which the people of Christ are united to Himself.

Faith is said to be our victory, for it brings us to Christ and so renders us victorious over the world which endeavors to keep us from Him; also, because it is the weapon of our warfare through which we obtain the victory. The world is the Christian's enemy, with which a combat is to be maintained and over which a conquest is to be won.

A true Christian has his enemies under his feet even while he is in the fight. He is a soldier as soon as he is a saint, and he is a conqueror as soon as he is a soldier. His very taking up arms ensures his victory.

The armor which the Christian is to use in his warfare is thus described: "Wherefore take unto you the whole armor of God, that ye may be able to withstand in the evil day, and having done all, to stand. Stand therefore, having your loins girt about with truth, and having on the breastplate of righteousness; and your feet shod with the preparation of the gospel of peace; above all, taking the shield of faith, wherewith ye shall be able to quench all the fiery darts of the wicked. And take the helmet of salvation, and the sword of the Spirit, which is the word of God: praying always with all prayer and supplication in the Spirit, and watching thereunto with all perseverance and supplication for all saints," Ephesians 6:13-18.

Those who have so many battles to fight and who, on their way to heaven, must dispute every step have need of great courage. Be strong, therefore—strong for service, strong for suffering, strong for warfare. Let a soldier be ever so wellarmed without, if he does not have within a decided heart his armor will stand him in little stead.

"Be strong in the Lord"—in His cause, for His sake, and in His strength. We have no strength of our own. Our natural courage is as perfect cowardice and our natural strength as perfect weakness. All our sufficiency is of God. In His strength we must go forth and go on. By faith, we must obtain grace and help from

God to enable us to do that which, of ourselves, we cannot do.

The soldiers of Christ, His saints, must be well-armed. Put on the whole armor of God. Make use of all the proper weapons for repelling the temptations and stratagems of the devil. Get and exercise all the Christian graces, the whole armor, so that no part is left uncovered and exposed to the weapons of this deadly enemy.

It is called the armor of God because God both prepares and bestows it. Nothing will stand us in stead but this armor; and, as it is prepared for us, we must put it on. We must pray for grace. We must use the grace given us and draw it out into action and exercise as there is occasion.

This the Apostle enlarges upon, showing us what our danger is and what need we have to put on this whole armor, considering what sort of enemies we have to deal with—the devil and all the powers of darkness. "For we wrestle not against flesh and blood." The combat for which we are to be prepared is not merely against our own corrupt natures, singly considered, but against the several works of devils who have a government and an influence which they exercise in this world, exciting the lusts and ministering to the pride and ambition of man. We have Satan against us, a subtle enemy who uses wiles and deceitfulness. He has many ways of beguiling unstable souls. Hence, he is called "a serpent" on account of his subtlety; an old serpent, experienced in the art of tempting.

The devil is a powerful enemy, having under him principalities, powers, and rulers, both numerous and vigorous, who rule undisturbed in those heathen nations which are yet in darkness, exercising a cruel dominion over all men who are yet in a state of sin and ignorance.

These enemies annoy the saints and strive to tempt them to sin. They strive to deprive them of heavenly ① blessings, to obstruct all their communion with God. ② They labor to deface the heavenly image in their ③ hearts. Thus, saints have need to be on their guard against the malice and subtlety of such foes. They have need of faith in their Christian warfare as well as of faith in their Christian work.

It is the Christian's duty to put on the whole armor of God.

Your duty, then, is to put on the whole armor of God and then to stand your ground against these enemies. You must not yield to the devil's allurements and assaults but decidedly oppose them. Satan is said to stand up against us. We must, therefore, stand up against him; set up and keep up an interest in opposition to his. Satan is the prince of this world, and his kingdom is the kingdom of sin. To stand against Satan is to strive against sin.

You should resolve, by the grace of God, not to yield to Satan. Resist him and he will flee from you; if you give way, he will get ground. If you distrust either your cause or your Leader, you give Satan advantage over you. Your calling is to withstand his assaults and to stand them out; and then, having done all that is incumbent on good soldiers of Jesus Christ, your warfare will be accomplished and you shall finally be victorious.

You should stand armed. The Apostle specifies the particulars of this armor, which is both offensive and defensive. Here is the military girdle or belt, the breastplate, the soldier's shoes, the shield, the helmet, and the sword. It is observable that, among them all, there is none for the back, as if to teach us the important lesson that if we turn our backs to the enemy we shall be exposed to danger and defeat.

Truth and sincerity is the girdle. It was prophesied of Christ that truth should be the girdle of His loins, and faithfulness the girdle of His reins. That which Christ was girt with, all Christians must be girt with. God desires truth, that is, sincerity, which indeed girds on all the other pieces of our armor. It is the Christian soldier's belt; ungirt with this, he is unblessed.

Righteousness must be our breastplate. The breastplate shelters the heart. The righteousness of Christ, imputed to us, is our breastplate to defend us against the arrows of sin. The righteousness of Christ, implanted in us, is our breastplate to fortify our hearts against the attacks which Satan makes against us. The Apostle explains this as "Putting on the breastplate of faith and love," 1 Thessalonians 5:8, which includes all Christian graces.

Shoes of brass, or the like, were formerly part of the military armor. The use made of them was to defend the feet against the traps and sharp sticks which were wont to be laid privily in the way to obstruct the marching soldiers.

The preparation of the gospel of peace signifies a prepared and resolved frame of heart to adhere to the gospel and abide by it, which will enable Christians to walk in a steady pace in the way of religion, notwith-

standing the difficulties and dangers that may be in it.
It is called the gospel of peace. It brings all sorts of
peace—peace with God, with ourselves, and with one
another.

Faith must be your shield "above all," or chiefly
"taking the shield of faith." Faith is all in all to the
Christian in the hour of temptation. The breastplate
secures the heart, but with the shield the Christian
warrior may turn every way. This is the victory over the
world, even our faith. Consider faith as it is, the evidence of things not seen and the substance of things
hoped for, and it will appear to be of admirable use for
this purpose. Faith—receiving Christ and the benefits
of redemption, and so deriving grace from Him—is
like a shield and a universal means of defense.

Now the devil is called the wicked one. His temptations are called darts because of their swift and undis-
cerned flight and the deep wounds that they give to
the soul; fiery darts, by way of allusion to the poisoned
darts made use of in ancient warfare. Violent temptations, by which the soul is set in fire of hell, are the
darts which Satan shoots at us. Faith is the shield by
which we must quench those fiery darts, whereon we
should receive them so that they may not hurt us.

Salvation must be your helmet, that is, your hope,
1 Thessalonians 5:8, which has salvation for its object.
This hope is an assured expectation of victory and
glory. The helmet secures the head. A good hope of
salvation, wellfounded, will be the means of keeping
the soul from being defiled by sin and of comforting
the soul and keeping it from being troubled and tormented by Satan. Good hope keeps the Christian trusting in God and rejoicing in Him.

The Word of God is the sword of the Spirit. The Word of God is very necessary and of great use to the Christian in order to his maintaining and succeeding in the spiritual warfare. It is called the sword of the Spirit because it is of the Spirit's creation, and He renders His Word efficacious, powerful, and sharper than a two-edged sword. It is the duty of the Christian to make himself acquainted with the doctrines, precepts, promises, warnings, and threatenings of the Word of God that he may be ready and able to give a reason for the hope that is in him, that he may be able to answer the opposers of the truth, to reprove sinners, and to comfort saints. Scripture arguments are the most powerful to repel temptation. Christ Himself resisted Satan's temptation with "It is written." The Word of God, being hidden in the heart, will be the means of preserving from sin and of mortifying and killing those lusts and corruptions that are lying hidden therein.

Prayer must buckle on all the other parts of the Christian armor. You should add prayer to all these graces for your defense against your spiritual enemies. You should pray always, without ceasing. You should keep up constant times of prayer and be constant to them. You should always keep up a disposition to prayer and intermix ejaculatory prayers with other duties and common business. You should pray with all prayer and supplication, with all kinds of prayer—public, private, and secret—with all the parts of prayer—adoration of God, confession of sin, petition for mercy, intercession for others, and blessings and thanksgivings for favors received.

You should pray in the Spirit. Your hearts should be employed in the duty, and you should do it by the

grace of the Spirit of God. You should watch thereunto, endeavoring to keep your hearts in a praying
frame and taking all occasions and improving all opportunities for the duty. You should watch all the motions of your hearts. You should persevere in prayer.
You should persevere in particular requests. You
should pray with supplication, not for yourselves only,
but for all saints, "For we are members one of another."

Thus should you become true soldiers of Jesus
Christ, answering to that double description given by
the Apostle John as mentioned before, "Whosoever believeth that Jesus is the Christ is born of God," and
again, "Whatsoever is born of God overcometh the
world, and this is the victory that overcometh the
world, even our faith."

How the enmity of the world acts against the souls of men.

The enmity of the world against the children of
God reveals itself in this way—it pretends to be a
friend, but its friendship is enmity. The friendship of
the world is enmity with God, James 4:4, and, therefore, is enmity against saints. Its kindnesses are darts,
swords, and arrows; its very peace is destruction to the
soul. We will now endeavor to show wherein the enmity of the world acts against the souls of men.

The world withdraws their affections from God as
their portion. And this is proved in the description
given in the Word of God of the worldly, the wicked
man, "the wicked will not seek after God: God is not in

all his thoughts," Psalm 10:4. <u>Men must either take
God as their portion or the world as their portion.</u>
    The world takes advantage of men's distempered
minds and appetites; it sets itself up as their god, as
their happiness or chief good. It proposes itself to
them for a portion, and that as their rich portion. It
tries to persuade men to satisfy themselves with what it
offers as a happiness, and that <u>it is unwise to seek an
unknown happiness at the risk of losing a present enjoyment,</u> which it will have to be the only happiness.
    Our blessed Lord invites poor sinners with these
gracious words: "Come unto me, all ye that labor and
are heavy laden, and I will give you rest. Take My yoke
upon you, and learn of Me; for I am meek and lowly in
heart; and ye shall find rest unto your souls," Matthew
11:28-29. "No, no," says the world, "stay with me. Dwell
here below. You see what your entertainment is here,
you know not what you shall find elsewhere. Here you
have substance. Here you have sunshine. Here you are
full and abound. You have your houses full, your hands
full, and your hearts full. You know what you have. You
can taste the sweets of enjoyment here. The treasures
of the other world, though they are called treasures of
light, yet to you they are but treasures of darkness. You
do not know what they are. Be content; <u>set your affections on things here below, where you are well off.</u>"
    The enmity of the world acts also against men's
souls in withdrawing them from their allegiance to
God as their Sovereign.
    When the world has once drawn away the heart, it
will easily pull away the shoulder. If the crown of God
is despised, His yoke will be quickly shaken off. Men
break faith with God when once they yield themselves

up to the world. If the world becomes their master, they yield themselves to it as servants. The strength of its temptations lies in the esteem they have for it and the affection they bear to it. Men will not bow before God when their hearts refuse to acknowledge Him, when they have chosen another god. What cannot the world lead them to if they have once made it their god! If it is their end, it will appoint them their means and way; any unrighteousness that will advance their worldly designs will be right in their eyes. Farewell faith, truth, mercy, honesty, and all consciousness of sin, further than they serve to make a gain of godliness.

The world, by withdrawing men from all love and obedience to God, exposes them to His wrath and displeasure. When they will have none of Him, He will have none of them. When they forsake Him, He sets Himself against them. God, in jealousy, says to those who profess to follow Him but who despise His name, "If then I be a Father, where is Mine honor? and if I be a Master, where is My fear?" Malachi 1:6. They who despise the riches of His goodness shall fall under His fury and fiery indignation. This is the state into which the world is leading men.

The enmity of the world acts against men by withholding them from Christ.

Christ came to bring sinners to God. As it is written, "For Christ also hath once suffered for sins, the just for the unjust, that He might bring us to God, being put to death in the flesh, but quickened by the Spirit," 1 Peter 3:18.

Four ways the world holds men back.

The world holds men back from coming to Christ by these four means:
1. By darkening their sight.
2. By deadening their senses.
3. By engaging their hearts.
4. By furnishing them with excuses for their neglect of Christ.

1. The world holds men back from coming to Christ by darkening their sight. It hinders men from perceiving the excellency of Christ or their need of Him.

Now the world, by raising mists of darkness, blinds men's eyes and prevents them from seeing the light of the glorious gospel of the Lord Jesus Christ. What is either beauty or blackness to the blind soul? We are naturally born blind; and, if our eyes begin a little to be opened, this world throws dust into our eyes that we may not see what is before us.

In the natural world, the sun dazzles men's eyes so that they cannot see the earth, but, in the spiritual world, the earth dazzles men's eyes so that they cannot see Christ, the Sun of Righteousness.

2. The world holds men back from coming to Christ by deadening their senses. Worldly men can neither see nor feel. They do not see the excellency and do not feel their need of Christ. They are infatuated by worldly vanities. They who live altogether by sense are without sense as to the value of any other than present things. They can contrive to live without Christ. The less they hear of Him, the better they are

pleased. They are opposed to Christ and His way, which is the way to poverty, not to wealth; to reproach and shame, not to honor. They can do well enough without Christ while they live, and what need they may have of Him after this life does not enter into their hearts. They are so busy with what they find here that they do not even look as far as the grave, much less beyond it.

It is hard to deal with such men except when they may be found alone, retired and withdrawn from the world. But how long may we wait ere we meet with such a season? Find them in a crowd among their worldly friends and companions, find them among their sheep or oxen, or find them at their pleasures, and the noise of these will so drown all that can be said that it will make no deeper an impression than a shower upon a stone. Cry an alarm in their ears, bring death and hell before them, and it does not move them even to ask such a question as: "What must we do to escape?" Men will never come to Christ till they see their need of Him; and they seldom see their need of Christ till, being withdrawn from the hurries of this world, they have leisure to reflect upon that which is to come.

Were men once deeply sensible how great their need of Christ is, how miserable, poor, blind, and naked they are without Christ, on what slippery places they stand, in what jeopardy they go daily, into what a dreadful gulf of woe and misery the wind and tide of their worldly prosperity are carrying them down, how suddenly they may be swallowed up in perdition and destruction, and what miserable comforts their past pleasures, and plenty, will then be to them; were they sensible that nothing but Christ, and union with Him will save them from the gulf—that laying hold upon Him, the Rock of Ages, can alone secure them from perishing; were they sensible that it is Christ alone who can secure them from danger, their need might be argument enough to drive them to Him. When the prodigal had spent all that he had in his riotous living, when his whole stock was wasted and not a husk left, then he had time to consider, and think to himself in what a condition he stood, and feel the pinching feeling of the necessitous state to which his folly had reduced him. This brought him to his senses; again, he came to himself and then away he went to his father.

3. The world holds men back from coming to Christ by engaging their hearts. The world gets hold of their hearts, and there it will keep its hold as long as their hearts yield to it. It gets so much within them, and so twists and twines itself about their affections, that it is very hard to separate them from it.

Men cannot, therefore, close with Christ unless they break off from the world. In those hearts where Christ gets possession, He casts out the buyers and sellers, and their merchandise out of His temple. He changes the customs, pleasures, and business of the heart. Its dealings and its delights, its affections and its labors, must no longer be bestowed and consumed upon meat and drink, and humor, dissipation and folly. Our gracious Lord gives other infinitely more delightful enjoyments and happinesses to those souls who are united to Him. He comes unto them and makes His abode with them, John 14:23. They are the objects of His dearest regard; they are the sheep and lambs of His flock, and He leads them into rich pastures.

The necessary businesses of life should be minded
in their place and season, but they must keep their
place. Stand off farms and oxen, stand off lands and
money, keep your distance. Christ will not come to be
an underling; He will have the chief respect and esteem; He will have the command of all that is in the
heart. Christianity consists in surrendering up the
heart to Christ. The question is not whether we can
find a corner in our hearts in which to entertain
Christ, but who occupies the throne, who has the government of the soul?

All sinful pleasures, all sinful gains, must depart
and come no more where Christ dwells; and those
which are lawful must come down and be brought into
subjection to Him. No more sensuality or worldly
mirth, no more covetousness or oppression, no more
pride or self-exalting, no more undue preference for
the lawful concernments of this life, no more unhal-
lowed anxiety about them, no more pleading business
against religion, no more pleading safety against duty,
no more pleading credit against conscience, no more
pleading gain against godliness; away with these, cast
them out, and never nourish these vipers again in your
hearts. All that of the world which you have had, which
you have ever loved, must become strange to you.
Rather say with the prophet, "Although the fig tree
shall not blossom, neither shall fruit be in the vines;
the labor of the olive shall fail, and the fields shall yield
no meat; the flock shall be cut off from the fold, and
there shall be no herd in the stalls: yet I will rejoice in
the Lord, I will joy in the God of my salvation,"
Habakkuk 3:17-18.

If men do begin to listen to the call of Christ, the

world steps in with its objections and asks, "What do you mean, simple souls? What are you doing? Where are you going? If you hearken to religion, to the Word of God, to your conscience, what will become of you? What will become of your property, of your honor, of your liberty? What will become of all the friendship and pleasure which you enjoy? Are you willing to be poor; are you willing to be in bondage; are you willing to be in reproach and disgrace? If you will have religion, and have anything to do with conscience, you are undone. Have you not given me your hearts; have you not cherished me, and cared for me as your own selves; and have not I deserved your care and respect? Have not I been the joy, and hope, and comfort of your lives? What will you be if I leave you, when your property leaves you, your pleasures leave you, your friends leave you?

"I know you love me. You love to be rich, to be great, to be at your ease; and you love your liberty as your lives. I know I have your hearts and you are unwilling to leave me. Therefore, consider and take heed, if you once hearken to religion and meddle with it, you will be dealing for another world, then farewell.

"But can you find it in your hearts to leave me? Has it not been well with you? Have you wanted anything? Have you not been filled with my good things? Have you not flourished and prospered? Have you not been full of meat and mirth, your bones full of rest, and your hearts full of ease and content? What have you lacked while you served me, and can you now find it in your hearts to part? Look to yourselves. On the day on which you resolve to follow religion, you must recollect and mark this, that I can become as bitter an enemy as

I have been a warm friend to you. I can persecute you and plague and vex you; and, if I may no longer walk in peace with you, I will be as thorns in your sides."

Again, the world argues, "Be advised, foolish souls, let us not part thus. Stay, stay with me. Do not go after you know not what. Do not forsake an old friend for a new. Believe it, the old friend will prove the better friend. If you will be wise, remain as you are and mind your present gain. Lay by the thoughts of the other world; let hereafter take care for itself. I have not been so good to you but that I can be better to you than ever. Come, do eat, drink, and be merry; gather, keep, lay up what is before you and cast away all care about a future world."

Thus, the world invites and flatters, beguiles and bewitches the soul into a neglect of Christ till it has smitten it to death and drowned it in perdition and destruction.

4. The world holds men back from coming to Christ by furnishing them with excuses for their neglect of Christ. Men are ashamed to be convicted of playing the fool, and they wish to have something to say for themselves to stop the voice of conscience and the mouths of men. It is written of those who were invited to the supper that they all, with one accord, began to make excuse. They were ashamed to say they would not come who had been too barefaced, but they excused themselves on account of their various occupations. Why, what is the matter that men will not come to Christ? What excuse have they? The world furnishes them with an excuse, just such a one as these men before-mentioned used: "I have bought a piece of ground, and I must needs go and see it. I pray thee

have me excused. And another said, I have bought five yoke of oxen, and I go to prove them. I pray thee have me excused. And another said, I have married a wife, and therefore I cannot come," Luke 14:18-20.

Dear friends, have your hearts never made this use of the world to excuse your neglect of Christ and your souls? It has, perhaps, hindered you many a time from coming to Christ, and then afforded you an excuse for not coming. How many prayers, how many Sabbaths, have you given up for it! Say, then, how much of these spiritual advantages has the world lost you? And when they are lost, when you have lost a praying time or hearing time, lost a Sabbath, a sermon, or a sacrament, has not this served as your excuse: "I was busy, and could not come"?

Our blessed Savior said to the Jews, "Ye will not come unto Me that ye might have life." Thus, in choosing death rather than life, you cannot say that you have reason on your side; therefore, no man can have reason to neglect Christ. No man can have reason to continue in sin; and, yet, there are few cases wherein men will not pretend to have reason for it, especially the worldling. He will be sure to find reason enough for his worldliness.

Though the drunkard will hardly say, "I have reason to be drunk"; though the covetous will hardly say, "I have reason to be an idolater"; though the swearer will hardly say, "I have reason to swear"; though the blasphemer will hardly say, "I have reason to blaspheme God," yet the worldling will readily say, "I have reason to get an estate, to keep what I have, to please my appetites, to enjoy the good things of this life, to look to self, and to enjoy what is my own."

Here, then, is the language of the worldling: "I pray you, have me excused." For what? That you do not come to Christ and hearken to and follow Him? That is, excuse me for undoing myself, for casting off all hopes of everlasting salvation, for going swiftly to hell.

Oh, what fools are the wise men of this world! They destroy their souls to please and provide for their bodies. They count the world their happiness; and this, their happiness, will ruin them. Some men's learning ruins them; some men's business has the killing of their souls; some men's money does it; some men's pleasures do it; some men's friends have the killing of their souls. Some are too rich, some are too busy, some are too merry, some are too high, some are too civil and courtly to come to Christ for salvation. Behold the wisdom of this world!

Inordinate, excessive care about the things of the world is vain and fruitless. Men weary themselves for vanity. Thus it is written, "Ye have sown much, and bring in little; ye eat, but ye have not enough; ye drink, but ye are not filled with drink; ye clothe you, but there is none warm; and he that earneth wages earneth wages to put it into a bag with holes," Haggai 1:6. And again, "Ye looked for much, and, lo! it came to little; and when ye brought it home, I did blow upon it. Why? saith the Lord of hosts. Because of Mine house that is waste, and ye run every man unto his own house," Haggai 1:9. The prayer of the saint was, "Turn away mine eyes from beholding vanity," and what else is there on earth to behold? What is there on earth which, when possessed, does not disappoint the expectation conceived of it? Solomon took an inventory of the world and of all its best things. He cast up the account, and the sum total which he made of it was *vanity.*

When our blessed Lord calls men to attend to a duty or an ordinance in order to bring them near to Him, and deals with them about their everlasting concerns—while some rejoice to come, to appear in His presence, to hear His voice, to pour out their souls to Him in prayer and praise—others are glad that they have something to say, that they could not wait on Him. They are glad of a business or a friend that kept them away; nay, even glad of a temptation that the devil laid as a block in their path, that the world called them out another way. They are more glad of a hindrance than of an opportunity, never considering what an eternal loss they may have thereby sustained.

Few seek Christ. His worship and service, His honor and interest are little regarded. The multitudes neglect Him. But why is Christ so neglected? Why, it is because every man is for himself and all seek their own, that is, their own outward and earthly things. "For all seek their own, not the things which are Jesus Christ's," Philippians 2:21.

Their own things—why are not the things of Christ as much their own as the things of the world? Are their worldly friends more theirs than Christ is? Are their earthly possessions, their earthly pleasures, their meat and their drink, their money, the things of their body more theirs than their soul and all its mighty concerns and interests? Men are but hypocrites if the things of Christ are not more theirs, more dear to them than the things of this world, if the things of Christ and their own things are not the very same to them. But unbelieving men count their worldly things to be their own things, and the more they seek their own, the less they value and seek the things of Christ. The most careful worldling is the most careless professor.

Dear friends, how little is done for Christ and how little is Christ sought after or served, let everyone judge themselves. Look back and sum up all that which you have done; bring together all concerning which you can say, "This has been done for Christ. This day, or this hour, was spent in seeking Christ and serving Him," and see into what a narrow compass all will be brought. Look into your hearts and see how many shops and fields you may find there in comparison with one sanctuary; how many markets and fairs have been kept there in comparison with one Sabbath. All that you have and are should be for the service of Christ. Every faculty should be His servant. Your thoughts, affections, understandings, consciences, hands, eyes, tongues should all be the servants of Christ; but are these at work for Christ? Are your understandings acknowledging Him? Are your thoughts searching after Him? Are your affections going out after Him? Are your consciences pleading for Him? Are your tongues speaking for Him? Are your hands laying up or laying out for Him? The devil has his servants busy working for him. Their worldly thoughts, their fleshly lusts, their earthly affections are all at work in his service to harden them against Christ, to entice them from Him, to defile and destroy their souls. But how little is done for Christ! It should make your hearts tremble if you were to consider how little!

What influence does Christ possess over your hearts? What faith, or love, or fear, or honor has He from you? How goes on His sanctifying work, His mor-

tifying work, in you? How fares it with His enemies in
you—your lusts, passions, and worldly affections? Are
not these still lording it over you? Then, consider how
little you have yet done for Christ; how little influence,
power, and authority He has over you; how low it is
with you both in point of grace and peace; how little
Christ is minded, or loved, or praised by you; how little
pleasure or delight you take in Him; how little care you
take for Him. How little has any good thing that He
has committed to you been cherished, nourished, and
improved? Does it not rather languish and pine away?
While your faces may shine, your state may flourish,
and your outward condition may thrive, in what a with-
ering state may your souls be!

Think with yourselves, are matters with you as you
could wish they were? Is it with your souls as Christ
would have it? Do you think He will acknowledge you
with that blessed sentence, "Well done, thou good and
faithful servant"? Have you been good stewards of His
manifold grace? How is it with you in outward things?
What are your duties? What are your ways? What praying, hearing, or working? Oh, rather, what shuffling
over duties, what halting in your goings! What do you
more than others? Are you not as worldly and vain as
others? Are you not as proud and froward as others?
Are you not as unprofitable as others?

Of what use are you to those among whom you
walk? What examples are you to them? Wherein are
they the better for you? Does your light shine? Do you
provoke others to love and good works? What do you
for your relations, for your friends, for your families, or
for any of the servants of Christ? Do you mourn for the
dishonor done to Christ with regard to His ministers,

His servants, His worship, His Sabbaths, and His ordinances? How does it fare with His gospel and with His
saints? Is all well? Is all at peace? Does the church
prosper? Does religion flourish, or does it not rather
suffer, mourn, and bleed? Yet who is there that cares
for any of these things? How few are they who lay them
to heart! Where are the hearts that tremble for the ark
of God, that ask how fares it with the Israel of God?

Oh, dear friends, it is lamentable to see how little
the things of Christ are minded. What is the reason?
Why, look abroad in the world and you may see reason
enough. Go into one town, go into another; go into
one place and another, and another. What are men
doing? How busy they are in buying, selling, building,
planting, plowing, and sowing, and in all matters belonging to this world. This is it, they are so busy for this
world that Christ, and the things of Christ, are little regarded by them.

The cares of this world choke the Word so that it
cannot prosper in worldly souls, so that it does not
quicken them, comfort them, or strengthen them. A
worldly-minded professor can never enjoy the hopes
and consolations which the children of God enjoy.
How many may we see among us who have lived a long
time under the profession of religion, have said that
they hoped in God, and had confidence that they be-
longed to Christ who, if they should take an account of
themselves and consider what advances they have
made in holiness all this while, what has been their
faith, their love, their zeal for God, their knowledge of
God, or their acquaintance with their own hearts—how
much humility, spirituality, and mortification, what
power over their corruptions, their pride, their pas-

sion, their peevishness, their worldliness they have obtained, what evidences they have gotten for heaven, what clearness and well-grounded confidence and assurance they are grown up to—might be persuaded that all this while they have been but unfaithful professors.

Alas! too, many a one may sadly say, "What have I gotten? How have I grown? Oh! have I not rather lost? Have I not rather fallen off? Is it not worse with me now than many years ago? It is not my faith, my love, my holiness, my hope, and my confidence that have grown; but rather my deadness and my sins that have grown upon me. I have less life, less love, less joy, and less peace than when I first thought of Christ."

Let worldly-minded professors consider whether such a lean, starving, and lifeless state of soul is not all the kindness that they have received from the world. Truly, it may have built their houses, bought their lands, filled their purses, fed their bodies, and provided for their families; but it has starved their souls. "Oh," may such a one say, "my leanness, my leanness, my dry and withered soul, my vile heart, my wasted conscience; how little truth or tenderness, how little love, life, or warmth do I feel within me! Oh, how much pride and frowardness, how much lust and liberty to sin has there grown upon me! I can fret, vex, and chafe; I can cheat, lie, and dissemble. All my vows and resolutions, after so long a time of profession, are not enough to restrain these vile abominations. O my soul, how sad it is with you! How low it is with you to this day! How does it come to pass? Why, this is your husbandry, your worldliness, your laboring so much, your hungering so much after the meat that perishes,

your being given to pleasure or to ease. This is what
has held you in such a poor case, such an unfruitful
and barren state, such a dark and uncomfortable state
as you are in at this day. For all this unhappiness, you
are beholden to the world and your worldliness."

It is strange that the world should ever prevail with
such strength as it does; that men of understanding,
endued with immortal souls, should ever suffer themselves to be led up and down as they are by such a per-
nicious and deadly enemy; that, when they have seen
so many lost and undone by it, they should never take
warning; that it should ever be trusted as it is, that it
should ever be loved as it is, that it should ever be
hearkened to as it is; especially when we consider how
unreasonable are its demands and how low and poor
are its rewards.

Suppose that the world should say plainly, "Come,
take your good things here and your evil things hereafter; take your riches in this world and your poverty in
the other world; take your pleasures here and plagues
hereafter. Be full, be merry, prosper, flourish, and rejoice for a few hours or for a few days, and be miserable, cry, howl, and be in torments to eternity."

If the world should speak out thus to men, by what
madness do you think those souls are bewitched who
would hearken to it? Though this is its design and men
might know it if they would but consider, yet, by far,
the greatest part of mankind are wandering after this
deceiver and are busy in making bargains with it to be
its captives and slaves. Yea, they not only suffer themselves to be persuaded and beguiled into this bondage,
but also willingly offer themselves as servants. "Take my
heart, O world," says one.

"Take my hopes," says another. "Let me but be a rich man. Let me be a great man. Let me have so much money, so much lands, so much pleasure, ease or honor. Let this moon shine upon me and take the sunshine, whoever will. Let me be this world's favorite and I am content to be its servant." And so along they go after it until they are lost forever.

What a wonder is this, and yet how many such prodigies are to be seen every day and in every place! This is the case of every worldling. You who will be rich, you whose hearts go after your covetousness, you who are given to pride, pleasures, or ease are boring your ears to the doorpost of your mortal enemy. You are selling your patrimony for husks. You are losing your souls and an eternal inheritance to buy, for a season, a house, a plot of land, some possession; nay, even a bundle of crackling thorns to make a blaze before which you may dance and be merry for a short time and, then, go down to everlasting darkness.

Wherein the strength of the world lies.

But wherein does the strength of the world lie? It lies in the natural enmity of the heart towards God which, degenerated and degraded by the fall of Adam, can alone be reclaimed by the grace of God and the sanctifying influence of the Holy Spirit. Thus has the world a strong party within man which sides with it; for, as in the whole generation of worldly men there is the same worldly spirit, so in the whole generation of the saints there is the same divine Spirit, the same Spirit of grace, the same Spirit of faith, the same Spirit of love, the same Holy Spirit. It is written, "We have received not the spirit of the world, but the Spirit which is of God," 1 Corinthians 2:12.

The spirit of this world is an earthly spirit. "The first man is of the earth, earthy," 1 Corinthians 15:47. In his creation, man had an earthy body; and, by sin, he is come to have an earthy soul. Sin was his fall from heaven to earth. As in the choice he made for himself, he chose an earthly inheritance; so in his temper, disposition, and tendency he, by nature, now inclines and bends towards earthly things. His soul, as well as his body, lusts after and feeds upon dust.

The spirit of the world is a short-sighted spirit. It cannot see afar off. Heavenly things are too far distant to be discerned by it. It loves, gapes for, and grasps things present; but the things to come, the things of God, are far out of sight.

The spirit of the world is a low and narrow spirit. These poor and beggarly things that this earth affords are the highest of its ambition.

Do you seek great things for yourself? What! Worldly goods? Are these the great things you seek—a great name, great estate, great possessions? You mistake, friends, these are but small things. They should be beneath the notice of a never-dying immortal soul. Meat and drink, mirth and money—are these the best things you find for your hearts to be set upon, for your souls to take pleasure in? You, who can take up with such things as these, do not have that mind in you which was in Christ Jesus.

The spirit of the world is a home-bred spirit. It has never been abroad but has been born and bred in this worldly region. It has never set foot upon, nor been acquainted with, a better land. The Spirit which is of God carries the soul to heavenly regions—to the regions of light and life, glory and immortality where it has made discoveries of other treasures, joys, and glories than are to be found here. The spirit of the world has ever dwelt at home. The souls of worldlings dwell in their houses of clay and never travel farther than this low earth. Their souls travel no farther than their bodies.

The spirit of the world has a suitableness to worldly things. This is the great advantage the world has over men. It tempts them to what they love and like. The world persuades them to follow their natures and their dispositions, to find there what will best please them, and there to take their fill.

But Christ calls and commands men to things and to ways contrary to their nature; not to please but to deny themselves, to mortify the flesh, to cross the appetite, to contradict their own inclinations; to pursue a happiness which is so sublime and spiritual and so unsuitable to their fleshly natures that they have naturally no relish for it. It is but here and there that one among many will be prevailed upon to hearken to Christ. To how many houses may faithful ministers come and to how many souls may they bring the everlasting gospel ere one will accept it? How many are called to Christ, to one who, in faith, comes!

Oh, dear friends, any of you who have cast off the world and have come to Christ are witnesses as to how hardly any of your souls were persuaded to come to Him, and how many there are who stand off, hang back, and will not be persuaded to come fully to Him. What is the reason for this? Oh, worldly men imagine that Christ calls them to their loss, persuades them to their hurt, that they have a better being, while they are wallowing in their riches and their pleasures, than ever they should find in following Christ!

Happy is he who, knowing what it is to prize the Savior and esteeming His blood precious, clings to Him in exact proportion as He reveals the depth of his own sinfulness. He is indeed a living stone in that building which will shortly appear in all its glory!

From the suitableness of the hearts of men to worldly things, they, first, readily take in of the world. Second, they greatly run out after the world.

They readily take in the world. The world knocks, and the heart gives it a ready welcome. The world offers, and the hand is ready to receive. Yea, though the terms upon which men must enjoy the world are ever so unreasonable, though for every draft of pleasure they must afterwards drink double in wormwood, though with the gains of the world they must drink in a curse—the dregs of the cup of the fury of the Lord and the dregs of the cup of trembling, Isaiah 51:17; yet, like men in a dropsy, though to drink will be death, their thirst they will quench.

It may be that conscience stands by and gives its warnings. It may suggest that there is poison in the cup, that there are serpents beneath the flowers, that a snare is spread in the loveliest paths; but still the heart is mad after its own delusions and, come what will, it must have the world for its portion, its treasure.

Men anxiously run out after the world. Oh, what haste they make to be rich! How their souls hunger and thirst after worldly greatness! They are as he who is thus described by the Prophet: "Yea also, because he transgresseth by wine, he is a proud man, neither keepeth at home, who enlargeth his desire as hell, and is as death, and cannot be satisfied, but gathereth unto him all nations . . . and heapeth unto him all people," Habakkuk 2:5. They enlarge their desire as hell. They have deep desires. They have large desires. They never have enough. "Their heart goeth after their covetousness," Ezekiel 33:31.

Now Christ is set before the eyes of men as an all-sufficient Savior who is the Bread of Life. Though the windows of heaven are opened and the fountains above broken up; though the durable riches, the everlasting pleasures of life, peace, rest, joy, and glory are set forth in open sight before the world; yet Christ, with His offered love, mercy, and kindness (and oh, how great is His love and mercy and kindness!), is despised and rejected by the world.

These are the words of the Psalmist: "The Lord looked down from heaven upon the children of men, to see if there were any that did understand and seek God," Psalm 14:2. God Himself is here described as an eyewitness. He is represented as looking down from heaven to show that He views the whole world and considers what all in it are doing. And in what a state does He find them? Behold, they are all running another way. There are none who understand, none who will seek God. Every worldly heart is closed against the warnings, the reproofs, the counsels, the threatenings, the promises, and the commands of God. "They are all gone aside, they are all together become filthy; there is none that doeth good, no, not one," Psalm 14:3.

What is the reason that your souls are such dwarfs, babes, and starvelings? Are they not so? Is it not very poor and very low with you? What treasures have you gotten? How little knowledge, faith, love, power, or vigor of spirit have you attained? How is death still feeding upon you—death in your understandings, death in your affections, death in your consciences, death in your duties? You walk up and down more like the shadows of Christians than like living Christians— pale and wan, weak and cold; mere carcasses of Christianity, wherein the soul and spirit of religion is not to be found. Look about, inquire among you, and see how many such dead carcasses there are to one living, lively soul!

The Lord be merciful to us! Though the name of religion is among us and upon us, yet the spirit of it seems to be greatly vanished away.

Dear friends, how is it with you who are now walking in the presence of the Lord? Turn in everyone his eye upon his soul and ask, "Soul, how fares it with you? How are you fed, O my soul? How are you clothed? What have you by you? What grace, what peace, what hope have you? Is not the world still preying upon and consuming you? Do you live, thrive, hold up your head, and hold on your way and your work, or are you not sick—head-sick, heart-sick, weak, poor, blind, and naked?"

Look within, each one of you, and take an account of your state. If you would do so, we do not doubt but that there are many who would find much within in a pitiful and lamentable condition.

What is the reason for all this? The Lord God has offered to feed and support your languishing souls. He would have nourished them up from babes to be men, from such weaklings to be strong in the Lord, but you would not. There is such an unsuitableness between the things of God and your worldly hearts that they have no appetite for them; whereas the things of the world find such a spirit of the world in them that, of anything that it has to offer them, nothing scarcely comes amiss. They not only readily take it in but greedily hunger and thirst after it.

Are there any of you, we would affectionately ask, who are setting up the idol-world in your hearts? If so, the frown of God is upon you, and that idol is destroying all peace and consolation. Enter, then, into the deep recesses of your hearts and seek out that beloved object which is possessed by your hearts. If they are not given up to God, they will be given up to the devil; and he will keep them to all eternity. Do not say that you cannot give your hearts to God. You can give them to covetousness, to drunkenness, to malice, nay, even to murder. You can give them to your lusts. Oh, how awfully can men deceive themselves!

How the devil tempts men.

The devil, as the prince of the world, tempts men:

1. By overrating the things of this world and underrating the things of the world to come.

2. By sharpening the edge of the evil things present and blunting the edge of the evil things to come.

3. By an active stimulating and exciting of the soul to pursue the present good and to escape the present evil.

1. The devil tempts men by overrating the things of this world and underrating the things of the world to come. The devil shows the world, in all of its glory, to those whom he tempts. He tempts men to take the

silver as gold, the brass as silver, stones as iron; he puts
upon everything a borrowed face that it may look better than it is. This was the deceitful promise which the
devil made to our first parents: "Ye shall not surely die,
for God doth know that in the day ye eat thereof, then
your eyes shall be opened, and ye shall be as gods,
knowing good and evil," Genesis 3:4-5. It is written,
"The god of this world hath blinded the minds of them
which believe not, lest the light of the glorious gospel
of Christ, who is the image of God, should shine unto
them," 2 Corinthians 4:4.

The crafty, deep design of Satan is to blind men's
eyes, knowing that they will not admire this world's
glory unless the eyes of their mind are blinded; but his
pretense is to open their eyes, to make such discoveries
of the presumed excellencies of earthly treasures as
will lead them to take earth for heaven.

Satan presents the world as that which has substance, sufficiency, contentment, ease, and satisfaction
in it. He will make promises of good things to his
friends and servants, as if he had all at his disposal.
And he finds men willing enough to believe him, for
the shadow becomes substance in those eyes which see
no better things.

Hence, earthly things are taken up by the men of
this world as their happiness, hope, and inheritance.
They take them as their portion in this life. The true
Christian says with the Psalmist, "And now, Lord, what
wait I for? My hope is in Thee," Psalm 39:7; but the
worldly man waits for, works for, and lives for the
world. He makes it his portion.

It is through the gospel that the glory of the other
world breaks in and shines down upon this. Here

Satan, the pretended opener-of-eyes, smites with blindness. He keeps the gospel, and all the glory of it, out of sight by a veil of unbelief. Unbelief seeks to give the lie to what the gospel speaks. It will even call into question, and hold under uncertainty, whether there is any such thing as the gospel or not.

What a low value worldly men put upon the all-important things of God, upon the great things of eternity! Glory, honor, immortality, and eternal life, what cheap things are these accounted by them, while soul and conscience, peace and hope, are so ordinarily sold by them to purchase an earthly inheritance! This is the bargain which they so eagerly drive after on this earth.

Would you learn to esteem the value of the soul? Weigh it by these words of our blessed Lord: "For what is a man profited, if he shall gain the whole world, and lose his own soul? or what shall a man give in exchange for his soul?" Matthew 16:26.

In the meantime, how few are there who will seek to gain heaven though it may be bought "without money and without price," though it may be had for the seeking, though it is brought to their hands, yet they will not take it. Now, Satan gains great advantage by his temptations, when the value of the world to come is so beaten down and when the value of the present world is so raised. As if the latter could hardly be overbought, and the former were scarce worth seeking after!

2. The devil tempts men by sharpening the edge of evil things present and blunting the edge of the evil things to come. The devil strives to make it appear that the afflictions of this life are more to be regarded than the judgment to come. He leads his slaves to think that

the persecutions of men are more to be feared than the anger of God; that there is no heaven or hell equal to those on earth; that poverty is more dismal than eternal fire, momentary disgrace than eternal condemnation, and the wrath of man than the curse of God.

Let death and condemnation be preached to worldly men, this stirs them not; let the devil tempt by tribulation, persecution, and man's fierce wrath, and how they are alarmed! Though the Word of God declares to them with such plainness and power, "He that believeth not shall be damned," Mark 16:16; "If ye live after the flesh, ye shall die," Romans 8:13; "For the wrath of God is revealed from heaven against all ungodliness and unrighteousness of men, who hold the truth in unrighteousness," Romans 1:18; "Who shall be punished with everlasting destruction from the presence of the Lord, and from the glory of His power," 2 Thessalonians 1:9—how little is this regarded! Who believes this report? How few are convinced, how few are awakened so as to consider how they may escape the wrath to come! Of how little avail, often, are all those arguments which are brought forward to turn men to flee from Satan and to seek Christ!

A cursing Shimei and a railing Rabshakeh will do more to frighten men from holiness than the consideration of the worm, the fire, the scorpions, and the torments of hell will do to drive them back from sin. They dare not to be saints for fear of the barking of dogs, but they dare to be sinners notwithstanding the roaring of lions. The devil has made such fools and such cowards of them that a few grains laid on them at present seem heavier than all the weight of all the punishment which the Almighty God inflicts upon sinners.

Third, the devil tempts men by an active stimulating and exciting of the soul to pursue the present good and to escape the present evil. If the devil can only persuade men that the present good things are so good that there is nothing better and the present evil things are so evil that there are none greater, he will gain a great advantage.

It is easy, as it is a common matter, for unregenerate men to profess that this world is a vain world, that its best goods and its best gifts are but vanity; and yet they will cleave to it. They will seek to make out a happiness in it by enjoying all that is in it which suits their corrupt nature, and avoiding all that is in it which is painful to that nature. They will put the bitter for the sweet and the sweet for the bitter. They will choose that which is evil for their good and they will refuse that which is good as a worst evil. Thus, their ways are not as the ways of God and their thoughts are not as the thoughts of God. Herein, we judge that they must be under the influence of the devil in the choice which they make.

But more particularly, the devil manages and quickens the temptations of the world by proposing objects and provoking the appetite.

First, by proposing objects he brings the world in sight. Sometimes he presents it immediately to the fancy. He raises great desires of the heart about it. He calls the thoughts abroad with him to take a view of the glory, the riches, and the pleasures of his kingdom. He sets men thinking on the pomp and fashions, on the gaieties and pleasures of the world, and rolling over in their minds the gains and sweetnesses of a worldly life.

Thus, he presents the world to the eye. There is a quick passage from the eye to the heart. If the devil can but turn the eye to behold vanity, by the eye he will easily infect the heart. He presents objects to the eye and he leads men up and down in the chains of their lusts where his baits and snares lie. Sinners are said to be led away with divers lusts, 2 Timothy 3:6. But where do men's lusts lead them? Why, everywhere, up and down. Some men's lusts lead them to their dissipations, to their sports and pastimes, to the public-house or tavern; other men's lusts carry them into the city, or into the field, or over sea and land, in order to find wealth and substance. Some men's lusts lead them to follow fashions, to get favor, and to climb up to dignities and high places.

Men need to consider what they go to and what their call is there. The devil more often has a hand in leading them up and down than they are aware of, and he who goes where the devil leads him falls into his snares. Men are never in more danger than when the hook is out of sight, and the bait is in sight. That is Satan's course, to hide the hook and to show the bait. He turned Eve's eyes to the apple, Achan's eyes to the wedge of gold, Ahab's eyes to Naboth's vineyard; and, then, what work did he make with them!

Second, by provoking the appetite. This he does by proposing such objects as are most enticing to those with whom he has to deal. The devil is skillful and wily. He understands the nature of the heart of man and the several inclinations that flow from it. Some men, he observes, are particularly of a sensual heart. For these, he has pleasures, mirth, gaiety, and dissipation.

The devil observes others to be of earthly minds,

gaping after wealth and riches. It is not mirth, gaiety, pleasures, and dissipation that will serve for these men. They must have substance. For these he has money, estates, fields, farms, and cattle. Such as this is the language of his temptations: "Will you be a rich man? Will you increase your stock and store? Will you enlarge your possessions? Hearken, look to yourself. Take care of yourself. Do not waste your time reading, praying, and hearing sermons. Mind your business and your interests. Set your heart upon your work and your work alone. Nourish not needless scruples. Away with all fears. The more free you are to venture on anything, the greater will your gain be. Let men or conscience clamor against you, all you earthworms, covetous, unjust, extortioners, and oppressors. Never mind them. You shall increase in substance, and that will make amends for all; and, as for conscience, if that is sore or troublesome, a little repentance, at last, will heal that."

It is written, "He also that received seed among the thorns is he that heareth the Word; and the care of this world, and the deceitfulness of riches, choke the Word, and he becometh unfruitful," Matthew 13:22. Care for the other world would, by the grace of God, quicken the springing of this seed, but care for this world chokes it. Worldly cares are well and fitly compared to thorns, for they came in with sin and are a fruit of the curse, Genesis 3:18. They are entangling, vexing, and wounding. A man must be well armed who deals with them. Worldly cares are one great hindrance to our profiting by the Word of God and to our proficiency in religion. They eat up that vigor of soul which should be exercised in divine things. They divert us from duty, they distract us in duty. They who are careful and cumbered about many things will neglect the one thing needful.

Oh, that men were sensible of this, that they are never so likely to starve as when they are resting upon their heaps, that their prosperous times are the devil's seasons to impoverish their souls, and that the abundance which is set before them is that temptation which the devil uses to entice their hearts after him!

Others are of airy spirits, proud and ambitious. These the devil tempts with the breath of popular applause, respect, esteem in the world, honor, and reputation.

Others are of a timorous and fearful heart. The devil deals with these in thunder and storms, threatenings, persecutions, bonds, banishments, reproaches, and cruel mockings. Such as this is the language of his temptations: "Look, you foolish creature, at what you are doing. See what rods are prepared for you. Are you able to stand against all the power of men? See how multitudes are joined against you and run upon you to devour you and swallow you up. Consider the rage of their hearts, the fury of their faces, and the violence of their hands. They are many, they are terrible, they are powerful, and they are near who seek your ruin. Awake from your folly. Do not help your own undoing. Save yourselves! Go and make your peace with them. Cast your lot among them and join with the multitude. Be as they are and let your ways be as theirs. Lay aside this pride and singularity and be as others, and it shall be well with you."

All the spies who were sent up by Moses, under the direction of the Lord, to view the land of Canaan, except Joshua and Caleb, made an evil report of that land. They said, "All the people that we saw in it are men of a great stature. And there we saw the giants, the sons of Anak, which come of the giants; and we were in our own sight as grasshoppers, and so we were in their sight," Numbers 13:32-33. Thus, the terror of these giants was upon the spies. Yet this very land, which they thought could not be conquered, and these very giants, whom they thought to be invincible, fell before the armies of Israel. Never let, then, the sons of Anak be a terror to Israel, to the people of God, for they must, in the end, fall. Giants become as dwarfs before the omnipotence of God and His saving strength, by which His people are led and guarded. Trials, afflictions, difficulties—these giants, to the view of feeble hearts, will fall before the Christian who is triumphant in faith.

Thus, craftily does the devil deal with every man according to the several tempers and dispositions of his heart; and his strength lies in his subtlety, and therein, depends his success. What wonder, then, is it that the fearful are frightened, that the proud are lifted up, that the greedy gape so wide, and that the full drafts of the world's stolen waters so easily go down with such whose souls are panting after them.

Our blessed Savior said to the Jews, "Ye are from beneath; I am from above: ye are of this world; I am not of this world," John 8:23. Here He showed the affection which these unregenerate and degenerate men had to the poor, low things of this world. The Spirit of the Lord Jesus was not of this world but from above. He was perfectly dead to the riches, honors, and enjoyments of this world. He was wholly taken up with divine and heavenly things, and none can be His disci-

ples here, or be partakers of His glory hereafter in
heaven, but those who are born from above and have
their conversation in heaven. How contrary to His
Spirit was the spirit of those men and any other such
men.

Dear friends, let us learn wisdom. Does the devil
take advantage of our tempers and dispositions and
order his temptations accordingly? Let us learn this
wisdom, to seek wisdom from God that we may know
our own hearts, observe our own inclinations, and,
accordingly, stand on our guard where we find this adversary most able to assault us.

Stand ever upon your watch, but especially when
there is anything before you that your poor hearts like
and are apt to fall lusting after. If ever you would fear
the devil, fear him when he is tempting your appetites
and passions. He never does you more mischief, perhaps, than when he is doing what appears to be good
to you. It never, perhaps, fares better with the children
of God than when they are crossed in their hopes, designs, and wishes; nor ever fares it worse with the devil's children than when they are humored and
honored. Never suspect the devil more than when he
pretends to do you a courtesy. Whatever it is by which
he usually pleases you, dread that as you would hell.
Mistake neither God's chastisements nor the devil's
kindnesses. Be content that God should afflict you and
cross you in your hopes and designs and be afraid
when the devil pleases you. Be convinced that God's
smitings are a precious balm and the devil's soothings
are stabs at your heart. Fear not Satan's thunder and
storms as much as his warm sun.

Thus, then, let the saint sing with a heart wholly

given up to God:

> Since 'tis Thy will, O Lord, that I should part
> With the most precious treasure of my heart,
> I freely that and all resign:
> My heart itself, and its delights are Thine.
> My little all I give to Thee;
> Thou gav'st a greater gift, Thy Son, to me.
> Take all, O gracious Lord, I will not grieve,
> But still will wish, that I had still to give:
> I hear Thy voice, Thou bidst me quit
> My paradise—I bless, and do submit;
> I will not murmur at Thy word,
> Nor seek a shelter from Thy chastening sword.

Where the strength of faith lies.

Now, let us consider wherein the strength of faith lies, whereby it overcomes the world.

The armies of the Israelites and Philistines being ready for battle, Goliath, a giant, came proudly forth to challenge the Israelites, saying, "Why are ye come out to set your battle in array? Am not I a Philistine, and ye servants to Saul? Choose you a man for you, and let him come down to me. If he be able to fight with me, and to kill me, then will we be your servants: but if I prevail against him, and kill him, then shall ye be our servants, and serve us. And the Philistine said, I defy the armies of Israel this day; give me a man that we may fight together," 1 Samuel 17:8-10. Now David accepted the challenge. Saul, the king, offered him his armor, but David would not wear it. "He took his staff in his hand, and chose him five smooth stones out of the brook, and put them in a shepherd's bag which he had, even in a scrip; and his sling was in his hand: and he drew near to the Philistine," 1 Samuel 17:40.

What a mighty enemy was this Goliath! Who was to stand before him? What was the stripling David to this giant? What was a sling and a pebble to a sword and a spear, to a helmet, leg coverings, and a target of brass! This proud Philistine came blustering, boasting, fuming, and chafing, so that he made the camp of Israel to quake. What could a poor stripling do to meet this mighty champion in battle? What hope was there of victory over him? We read further:

> And the Philistine came on and drew near unto David; and the man that bare the shield went before him. And when the Philistine looked about, and saw David, he disdained him: for he was but a youth, and ruddy, and of a fair countenance. And the Philistine said unto David, Am I a dog, that thou comest to me with staves? And the Philistine cursed David by his gods. And the Philistine said to David, Come to me, and I will give thy flesh unto the fowls of the air, and to the beasts of the field. Then said David to the Philistine, Thou comest to me with a sword, and with a spear, and with a shield: but I come to thee in the name of the Lord of hosts, the God of the armies of Israel, whom thou hast defied. This day will the Lord deliver thee into mine hand; and I will smite thee, and take thine head from thee; and I will give the carcasess of the host of the Philistines this day unto the fowls of the air, and to the wild beasts of the earth; that all the earth may know that there is a God in Israel. And all this assembly shall know that the Lord saveth not with sword and spear: for the battle is the Lord's, and he will give you into our hands. And it came to pass, when the Philistine arose, and came and drew

> nigh to meet David, that David hastened, and ran toward the army to meet the Philistine. And David put his hand in his bag, and took thence a stone, and slung it, and smote the Philistine in his forehead, that the stone sunk into his forehead; and he fell upon his face to the earth. So David prevailed over the Philistine with a sling and with a stone, and smote the Philistine, and slew him; but there was no sword in the hand of David. Therefore David ran, and stood upon the Philistine, and took his sword, and drew it out of the sheath thereof, and slew him, and cut off his head therewith. And when the Philistines saw their champion was dead, they fled.
>
> (1 Samuel 17:41-51)

The strength of Israel was David; the strength of David was his faith; the strength of his faith was the name of the Lord. He came to the battle in the name of the Lord of hosts. "The name of the Lord is a strong tower: the righteous runneth into it, and is safe," Proverbs 18:10.

But, to come closer to the matter, we shall urge two particulars: 1. The strength of a Christian is his faith; and 2. the strength of faith is Christ.

1. The strength of a Christian is his faith. "All things are possible to him that believeth," Mark 9:23. There is nothing impossible to faith, because there is nothing impossible to God. You will find the eleventh chapter of the Epistle to the Hebrews to be a short chronicle of the mighty power and influence of faith. Faith spoiled death of its prey, as in the case of Enoch, Hebrews 11:5. His faith carried him to heaven by a new way. He was translated and did not see death. Faith makes an ark to save from the flood, as in the case of

Noah, 11:7. Faith led one to leave his own country, not knowing where he went, as in the case of Abraham, 11:8. Faith received a living child from the dead by offering him up to death, as in the case of Isaac who was offered up to God by his father Abraham, 11:17-19.

But more fully to our purpose, faith overcame the world. Faith despised and rejected the prosperity of the world. It is written in this chapter, concerning those holy men of old who were not mindful of their earthly country, that they desired a better country, even a heavenly one, and were content to be strangers and pilgrims in this world that they might become possessors of that better country, even a heavenly one, that better inheritance. Their country was on the other side of the Jordan, and there they sent their hearts, 11:16. Moses, by faith, forsook the glory of Egypt and the court of Pharaoh, choosing rather to suffer affliction with the people of God than to enjoy the pleasures of sin for a season, 11:25. By faith, saints choose the good part, Luke 10:42, and lay hold on eternal life, 1 Timothy 6:12.

Faith describes a better country. It sees into the invisible world. Finding it to be a good land, there the faithful servant of Christ resolves to take up his rest. He says, "The Lord is my portion forever. In Him is my salvation. If I can but make my way through this weary land, and at last enter into the heavenly rest, if I can but attain to the resurrection of the just, and be with Christ, that is all my desire and design."

Meet a believer where you will and ask him, "Where are you bound?"

He can say, "Oh, for the heavenly country."

"Whom do you seek?"

"Jesus of Nazareth."

"What are you running for?"

"The incorruptible crown."

Ask him again, "Will nothing less content you? Look about through all the earth, can you find nothing worthy of your esteem? Are silver, gold, houses, lands, and pleasures nothing to you? May not these satisfy you?"

"No, no," he will say, "these do not make my heaven. There is no rest here for the sole of my foot. My house and my home is above; my hope and my treasure is above and my soul is above and cannot be content to grovel in the dust."

Ask him yet again, "But how will you ever enter into that good land? There are difficulties and dangers in the way. You have a wilderness to go through, a Red Sea and a Jordan to pass over. There are lions in your way. You may be a prey to your enemies or, at least, you may wander in the wilderness, lose your way, and never come into your rest at last."

"Well," he can answer, "I must venture, I am resolved for heaven. However difficult or dangerous the way may prove, I will venture all here; heaven or nothing. This heart can never be at rest till I be with Christ where He is."

Faith triumphed over the power and wrath of the world. It subdued kingdoms, wrought righteousness, quenched the violence of fire, escaped the edge of the sword, out of weakness was made strong, turned to flight the armies of the aliens, endured cruel mockings and scourgings, yea, moreover, bonds and imprisonments; endured stoning, sawing asunder, wandering about in sheepskins and goatskins, in a destitute, afflicted, and tormented condition. In all these things, the servants of God were more than conquerors through faith in Christ who loved them.

Thus, faith gives a right judgment of the world. By faith, we understand what is the worth and power of the world, what it can do for us or against us; and we understand its end too, of what duration it is as well as its beginning.

Faith takes its estimate of the world from the Word of God and gives its judgment of it according to that Word. This Word speaks of everything as it is; of God as He is, of sin as it is, of the present world as it is, and of the world to come as it is. What this Word speaks God speaks; and, whatever faith speaks, it has it from the Word of God.

Oh, how many captives has the world taken! What multitudes of prisoners has it made! Some it has bound in golden chains and fettered in riches and worldly gains, in honors and dignities. Some it holds as with a spider's web, such as the fashions and fooleries of the world with its pomps, pleasures, and humors. Others it has laid fast in iron chains, manacled with fears and dread of its fury and violence. They dare not be saints, they dare not appear in the armor, lest they should be known as disciples of Christ; but they dare to be sinners, to be haters of Christ.

How many renegades and apostates has the world made, who have run from their colors and have listed themselves under the devil, under whose conduct they are fighting against that faith and holiness which they have perhaps professed!

Alas! How few faithful ones are left, and those who are, how afraid are they of sufferings! How cold and

spiritless are they in the way of duty! It is woeful to observe with what a pale face Christianity looks out at this
day, but it shall not always be so. The Lord shall, in His
own time, trample the enemies of His cross underfoot
and establish His true religion in all the radiance and
brightness of its glory.

Ah! Poor souls, how many are there whose peace is
slain, whose comforts are slain, and the spirit of light
and life within them vanished into dimness and darkness; and all this because their faith has so much failed.
They mourn and say, "What have we become and to
what a low ebb are we brought, O we of little faith!"
Well, there is hope even in this state. This stump, there
being life in the root, will spring again and recover
again. You who have but a little faith, blow on the living spark, and your sick, despoiled, and half-dead souls
will yet revive again. If your faith, once out of weakness,
is made strong, it will recover all you have lost.

Nourish, cherish, and exercise faith more. Lean on
Christ who gives strength to His people by His Spirit.
Look unto Jesus, lay hold on the covenant, live upon
the word of promise, and feed upon the fullness of the
Lord. Recollect that "man shall not live by bread alone,
but by every word that proceedeth out of the mouth of
God." Let your faith gather strength again, and this will
be the strength of your hearts. It will renew your life,
rekindle your love, enflame your zeal, set your holiness
and your hopes again upon the wing, and bring the
world and its temptations again under your feet. Thus
the strength of a Christian is his faith.

2. The strength of faith is Christ. Christ is the
Mighty One, the Mighty God, Isaiah 9:6; the Lord
Jehovah in whom is everlasting strength, Isaiah 26:4.

Through faith, this mighty God is our God and this Rock of ages is our Rock.

By virtue of union with Christ, there is a diffusion of the strength of Christ into the souls of His people. Thus, the Apostle prayed for his Christian brethren, "For this cause I bow my knees unto the Father of our Lord Jesus Christ, of whom the whole family in heaven and earth is named, that he would grant you, according to the riches of his glory, to be strengthened with might by his Spirit in the inner man; that Christ may dwell in your hearts by faith; that ye, being rooted and grounded in love, may be able to comprehend with all saints what is the breadth, and length, and depth, and height; and to know the love of Christ, which passeth knowledge, that ye might be filled with all the fulness of God," Ephesians 3:14-19. As true Christians have the mighty protecting hand of Christ over them, so they have the mighty Spirit of Christ in them whereby they wax strong in the Lord and in the power of His might.

O faithful servants of the Lord, it is Christ who is in you. Who is he that is in the world? The devil is in the world. Christ is greater than Satan, this adversary; and, therefore, you shall overcome. Now, he who is in the world is great, but He who is in you is greater. He who is in the world is strong and crafty, but He who is in you is stronger and wiser. What is a company of poor children to a mighty giant? But, behold, Christ is the children's champion, and you will quickly see on which side the victory will go. Who is he who has overcome? Your Captain, your Champion, has overcome, and overcome for you. He has overcome, and you in Him. It is written, "Nay, in all these things we are more than conquerors through him that loved us," Romans 8:37.

Our blessed Lord and Savior gives strength to the faith of His people. He has power to prevent temptation. It is written, "There hath no temptation taken you but such as is common to man; but God is faithful, who will not suffer you to be tempted above that ye are able; but will with the temptation also make a way to escape, that ye may be able to bear it," 1 Corinthians 10:13.

Our blessed Lord and Savior has all our tempters and temptations in His power—the devil in His power; the world in His power. They must have leave ere they can act. If He says the word, the Assyrian shall not come against Jerusalem, nor shoot an arrow there, nor cast a bank against it. God has His hook in the nose and His bridle in the lips of all His enemies, 2 Kings 29:28-32.

Our Lord Jesus Christ has power to deaden temptations, to take the edge off those who, though they may touch, yet they shall not enter; though Satan strikes, yet his arrows shall not pierce. Christ, by His cross, has slain the world. It has now become, to watchful saints, as a dead thing; its beauty and glory is dead, dried up and withered. Christ, by His cross, has revealed the glory of the other world. Life and immortality are shown forth in open sight on the cross of Christ, and that sunshine has withered all the flowers here below. Who will be taken up with trifles who see, by faith, the crown of glory which Christ has set before their eyes? And as the beauty and glory, so the power and wrath of the world is slain. Christ, by His death, slew all the powers of darkness. A Christian sees that the world can now do him neither good, by its friendships, nor hurt, by its malice. Who would be enticed by a dead carrion or affrighted by a dead lion?

Christ has slain the world without and the worldly lusts within his saints. The Apostle thus wrote, "Knowing this, that our old man is crucified with him, that the body of sin might be destroyed, that henceforth we should not serve sin," Romans 6:6. And again, "For ye are dead, and your life is hid with Christ in God," Colossians 3:3—dead to this world and dead to things below. The Apostle said that he was crucified unto the world; that is, worldly temptations were no more to him than if he were a dead man. What are meat, drink, clothes, pleasures, and honors to a dead man? If one should go preach among the tombs and call out to the dead, "Hearken to me, and I will feed you with delicacies, clothe you in purple, enrich you with silver and gold, exalt you to honor," what skull or bone would be moved? Were he to offer them gold and silver, what hand of theirs could clench them? Thus, the devil would in vain tempt men, were they really dead to the world. The highest temptations would move them no more than a body in the grave.

Our Lord Jesus Christ has power to succor those who are tempted. Though the tempter is let loose and temptations come thick and strike deep, our experiences sadly testify how much the world is often too hard for us, how often we are entangled and led away by it; what inroads it makes on our peace; what wounds in our hearts, and what fears and misgivings hereupon arise in our souls as to how we shall stand for the future. Thus we are weary, distressed, and hard put to it, yet though it is thus with us in the midst of all these, there is this to support us: "For in that He Himself hath suffered being tempted, He is able to succor them that are tempted," Hebrews 2:18.

Our Lord Jesus Christ has power over the world to restrain it from tempting, to deaden its temptations, to succor those who are tempted; yea, more than that, He has already overcome the world, and thereby secured the final victory of His people. These are His own words: "In the world ye shall have tribulation; but be of good cheer; I have overcome the world," John 16:33. Here, O saints, is comfort and encouragement for you, that your enemy is not invincible. He has been beaten and will be beaten. There is this further comfort for you, that in Christ's victory, you have overcome.

As all the power of Christ is engaged for the help and assistance of His people, they are interested in His victory. Christ's victory is their victory. He is concerned to protect and help them. His people are His own. The attempts that are made against them are made against Him. As in all their afflictions He is afflicted, so their enemies are His enemies. Is not Christ concerned to look to His own? He is. Then may the disciple of Christ say, "I am Thine, save me; I am Thy child, Thy servant, a lamb of Thy flock. Thou art my Shepherd. I have committed myself to Thee, and Thou hast undertaken for me."

Do you profess to be Christians? Then where is your faith? Do you say that you have faith while you know not Christ? Must not the world bend before Christ? Do you profess that you are born of the Spirit and yet say, "I cannot help it to be thus earthly-minded"? Mistake not yourself, you have reason to fear lest your "cannot help it" becomes a "will not help it," or a "care not to help it."

Are you not too anxious for this vain world? You are

inexcusable, O man who pleads inability, when Christ is ready to give strength and power to those who ask for it in faith. Jesus said unto one who prayed Him to cure his son, "If thou canst believe, all things are possible to him that believeth," Mark 9:23.

By faith, we understand that the prosperities of the world cannot further, and the troubles and trials of the world cannot hinder, man's eternal happiness.

Men are apt either to be pleased or dissatisfied with the various matters which they meet with according as they serve or cross their aim and end. He who has made eternal glory his aim and end values things according as they tend heavenward. It is a sign that men have made the world their aim and end when worldly objects and occupations are the things they are taken with, and everything is a cross that touches upon their worldly interests. What would promote their eternal interests, they are satisfied to live without; what is a hindrance to their souls, they can bear and find no trouble, but what serves or disserves their selfish interests are the things that move them. Let such souls never talk of making eternal glory their end. If that were their end indeed, if they were for heaven in earnest, then what will please God and what will lead to heaven would be the only things which their hearts would anxiously seek after.

The prosperities of the world cannot further man's eternal happiness. There is no man who is nearer to heaven for being rich or honorable. Believe it, friends; to be rich in this world and to be rich towards God are two different matters. The great things of the world may undo you; your gold may sink you; you may break your necks from off your high pinnacles; your temporal prosperities may shut you out from the everlasting kingdom and may be the death and condemnation of your souls, but never the salvation of them.

On the other hand, the troubles and trials of this world cannot hinder your eternal happiness. Faith sees as open and near a way to heaven from the lowest spot on earth as from the tops of the mountains, from the prison as from the palace, from the cross as from the crown. The gate of heaven shall never be shut against any because he is poor or persecuted. It is not a purple robe or a gold ring that shall procure entrance, nor rags, sores, or reproaches that shall shut the door.

There is a reason why the saints of God keep away from the world and the things of it, as there is why unbelievers keep away from God and the things of God.

Worldly men can lack the presence and favor of God, live without religion and the duties and comforts thereof, and never miss them. Why so? Because these things do not at all serve their design. They can be rich, great, and happy without minding God, or holiness, or their salvation. A true and faithful Christian can bear the lack of luxuries or any of his outward comforts. Why so? Because these, if he had them, would not serve his purpose.

By faith, we understand that the design of temptations is to deprive man of his inheritance. A true Christian knows that the devil owes him no good will and he sees that all his promises are cheats, that his gifts are bribes to corrupt him first and then destroy him. He marks him for his mortal enemy whose drift is to keep him out of heaven. He has learned from the Scriptures who it was who at first caused man to be thrust out of paradise—this serpent was he, Genesis 3.

And he observes how Satan's particular temptations serve his general design to destroy souls. Whatever the voice is, the true meaning of every temptation is that the soul may be led away from God.

Faith understands what use the devil has made of the world. Where did the rich man's purple, fine linen, and delicious fare lead him? If he had been seen in the state he was in, clothed in his gorgeous apparel and seated at his voluptuous table, a worldly heart would have blessed him saying, "Oh, this is a happy man!" But where do we find him? Oh, how sadly is the scene changed! Behold, this rich worldling in hell torments! A true Christian would have seen him near hell, at first view, while in the midst of all his luxury and gluttony.

The Psalmist, speaking concerning the wicked, says, "When I thought to know this, it was too painful for me, until I went into the sanctuary of God; then understood I their end," Psalm 73:16-17. When he went into the sanctuary of God to read or hear the Word of God and to spread his case before God in prayer, then he was enabled to understand the end and final doom of prosperous sinners.

How was it with them when he saw their end? Where were they? Why, in the midst of all their prosperity, in the height of their pride, in the full gratification of their lusts, amidst the heaps of their wealth, fat and flourishing, as full of mirth and gaiety as their hearts could wish, and without any fear of a fall. Even then he saw their end and that he had no reason to envy them. In their very noontide, he perceived their night. But what end was it he saw these men would come to? It follows in the next verses: "Surely thou didst set them in slippery places: thou castedst them down into destruction: How are they brought into desolation, as in a moment! They are utterly consumed with terrors." That was the end which he saw was hastening upon them—desolation and destruction.

Oh, dear friends, do you see the proud, insulting, oppressing world? Do you see the poor worldlings scrambling for wealth, climbing up to honor, dividing the spoils and sharing the riches and the preferments and pleasures of the world among themselves? Beware that you envy them not. Look a little farther and you will see no basis for envy but for pity and praise; pity for them who are but fattening for the slaughter, and praise to the Lord on behalf of yourselves that your souls are not gathered with them.

Faith understands, from the many instances it finds in Scripture, what mischief and ruin the devil has hereby brought upon souls; and, when this is understood, then the bewitching face of the world, notwithstanding all its paint, may not look so beautiful and amiable in your eyes.

Faith gives a better assurance of the better inheritance which is reserved for the people of God. "Faith is the substance of things hoped for, the evidence of things not seen," Hebrews 11:1. It is an evidence not only that there is another world, but also a better world than this, and that this better state may be obtained; that there is an entrance into the everlasting kingdom; that this mortal shall put on immortality; that this corruptible shall put on incorruption; and that poor worms that creep in the dust may get wings and fly away hence into everlasting bliss. It is also an evidence that there shall be a performance of all those glorious things which God has spoken concerning His saints.

The true Christian is not only interested in Christ and what He has done, but that Christ is in him; the Spirit of Christ, which is the Spirit of the living God, is in him. It is written, on the other hand, "If any man have not the Spirit of Christ, he is none of His," Romans 8:9. The same power by which Christ overcame is communicated to the souls of His people, and, hence, may they be said to have already conquered because they have received the aid of the Spirit, which will certainly work for them the victory.

True Christians are actually interested in Christ's victory. Whatsoever Christ has done as Redeemer of the world has been done for His people. The Apostle Paul thus wrote, "Therefore let no man glory in men. For all things are yours; whether Paul, or Apollos, or Cephas, or the world, or life, or death, or things present, or things to come; all are yours; and ye are Christ's; and Christ is God's," 1 Corinthians 3:21-23. True Christians belong to Christ; therefore, all good belongs to them and is sure to them. All is theirs—time and eternity, earth and heaven, life and death—because they are one with Christ, being His purchased and redeemed servants, and Christ is one with the Father; so, as the glory of God is displayed in Christ the Son, the salvation of the saints is secured in Christ their Head who will make them conquerors and give them a glorious victory over sin and Satan. Christ's victory is His people's security.

But let not any, merely because they profess to be Christians and through the forms of religion, persuade themselves that they are conquerors. It is written, "Who is he that overcometh the world, but he that believeth that Jesus is the Son of God?" 1 John 5:5. And it is declared that Christ "became the author of eternal salvation unto all them that obey Him," Hebrews 5:9.

What can an infant do? He is weak as water. He cannot speak, he cannot stand, and he cannot conquer a fly. But what may not this child do when he is grown up? There is the spirit of a man in him. There is a soul in him which, in time, may effect great things. Neither can a dead child do anything, nor is there hope that he ever should; but a living child has a soul, he has that within him which, in time, may do much.

How small are the appearances of the saints in the infancy of their new birth! How low are their hopes that they should ever come to anything! A weak enemy and a weak assault appears too strong for them. A little wind may blow away a small twig, but despise not this day of small things. Consider that the root of their strength is the Spirit of Christ which is in them, and then you may expect great things.

Are there any of you who are grown Christians, strong in the Lord and in the power of His might, who are able for service and mighty for sufferings; who can stand against the temptations of Satan and endure the contradictions of sinners and not be weary and faint in your minds? Look back and consider what you were in your newborn state. Time was when you were as weak as others, when you were as faint and weak as the weakest; but behold what that mighty Spirit has done for you, the same Spirit which is in every newborn saint, in every child of God.

How small and weak were Joshua, Gideon, and Samson when they were children! But when they were grown, and the Spirit of the living God came upon them, what victories did they obtain? The sons of Anak and the armies of the Philistines were but as children to them.

You who are yet little children, but of little time and little strength and who are newly born of the gospel and cast upon a tempestuous world, let not the greatness of your work, nor the power of your enemies, nor those astonishing tempests that meet you at the threshold of Christianity discourage or dismay you, as weak as you are, as many fears and faintings as you are surprised by, and with as many doubts as arise in your hearts. You perhaps say, "What shall I do? How shall I stand? How shall I go through and conquer all these enemies of my soul and salvation?" Yet comfort yourselves with these words: "Ye are of God, little children, and have overcome them: because greater is He that is in you, than he that is in the world," 1 John 4:4.

The great design of the world is to keep saints from Christ. Herein stands the deadly enmity of the world against souls, in holding them under its dominion and, thereby, under the condemnation of hell. When saints are once come over to Christ, this great design is broken. When they are conquered by the power of the Holy Spirit, they become conquerors. A soul subdued unto Christ is the world conquered in the soul. Every convert to Christ is a captive set at liberty, a soul released from prison. This is the word which Christ had to preach: "Say to the prisoners, Go forth; to them that are in darkness, Shew yourselves," Isaiah 49:9. And this is the work which Christ had to do: "To bring out the prisoners from the prison," Isaiah 42:7.

Oh, the sweet and happy liberty of the children of God! All the world besides them are very slaves and lie exposed to the bolts, fetters, and scourges of their hard and malignant master, the devil.

What is liberty but freedom from bondage? Behold, the Christian's freedom from the bondage of sin ties him to a sure liberty, which is his free obedience to God. See how free the good man is. He does what he will, for he wills according to the will of God, what God would have him to will. Neither has any man a free will to do good but he. Be then ambitious of this holy, happy, and lightsome condition, O you noble and generous Christians! Follow on more and more to attain this true liberty, "the liberty wherewith Christ hath made us free," Galatians 5:1.

It is a sufficient proof that you are worldlings still if you are not converts to Christ. He who is come to Christ is come out from the world, and he who is still under the yoke of the world is not come to Christ.

When the heart is convinced that there is no compounding between Christ and the world and, hereupon, yields itself to Christ saying, "Lord, I am Thy servant and will follow Thee whatsoever becomes of me, whether I want or abound, prosper or suffer. Whatever my condition is here, Thine I am, and Thee will I love and serve." When the heart has come to this, there is conversion; and there the great design of the world is broken.

The true Christian is marching on.

The true Christian is effectually marching on in pursuit of his victory. He keeps his enemy in his eye, is cautious and watchful, and dispatches messengers—his prayers, his sighs, his tears—to bring down fresh supplies from above. His prayers speak, his sighs cry, his tears have a tongue, and all go up with the same message.

He sets all his graces, his faith, his love, his hope, his patience in battle array against the world.

He is still gaining an advantage over the world. He, through the grace of God, strives against sin and keeps pride, covetousness, and sensuality down. He secures the stronghold. He, through grace, keeps the wealth, honors, and enjoyments of the world at the greatest distance. He sends his heart far enough away out of their reach into the other world, where it dwells; and he lays up a better treasure, where it rejoices and recreates itself, where it has far better work, better company, and better enjoyments than any here below. He lives in the view and contemplation of God and is so satisfied with the Fountain of living waters that he is neither thirsty after the waters nor choked with the mud of the broken cisterns of the world.

He studies the world more and comes to a better understanding of its vanity, enmity, treachery, crooked policy, and ruinous power; and the more he knows it, the more he fears it. The more he knows of God, the more he loves, pants, and longs after Him. The more he knows of the world, the less he loves it and the more he fears it. He fears not so much its anger as its kindness. He has a jealous caution of worldly pleasures, worldly businesses, and his prospering in them. He carries a sense of the danger he is in by them and a fear of the dangerous snare they may be to him in his way while he is necessarily detained and busied here. He carries this caution as his guard to secure his soul wherever he goes—to his table, to his shop, to his farm, or in his journeys. He feeds with fear, works with fear, travels with fear, and trades with fear; lest, while he is thus necessarily conversant in the world, he is again entangled with its temptations.

In this warfare, he advances and gathers strength daily; he is more able to despise the world, and it becomes less and less a temptation to him. Time was when, whenever the world came persuading, enticing, or threatening him, these were arguments of great weight with him. They could command his heart, control his conscience, lay hold on his affections, and turn him one way or another. But now his heart is set upon securing his eternal interest and transported with the sense of the importance of those higher things of eternity. They are so great in his eyes and so much upon his heart that it seems but a small thing to him to be possessor of many things here and seems to make but a small difference in his feelings and views whether he lacks or has possessions.

Victory consists in the Christian's relationship to the world.

The victory which the children of God gain, by the grace of God, over the world, consists in a power to possess the things of the world without placing their happiness in them.

The supremacy of the world is founded in its supposed power and sufficiency to bless men and to make them happy. While men hold it as their treasure, they resign themselves to it as their ruler. The heart will never dwell in, or serve, the world when it has chosen another treasure. The world can never hold the do-

minion of a lord longer than it can hold the reputation
of being the chief good. The soul will not be governed
or commanded by it, unless it is determined to take it
as its reward. When the heart has said to the Lord,
"Thou art my portion," it can say to the world. "Stand
aside, I have nothing to do with you." When men neither promise themselves contentment in their expecta-
tions nor feel at rest in their possessions, when the
heart is fixed on God and so strongly working upward
that it will not be detained from the service and worship of Him by anything it either has or hopes for
here, then the world is vanquished.

Again, the victory which the children of God gain,
by the grace of God, over the world consists in a power
to manage their worldly affairs without damage to their
souls.

The servants of God should pay attention to those
duties in life to which God calls them. The plow must
be followed, the seed must be sown, the flocks must be
kept; kings and subjects, masters and servants, princes
and peasants should all fulfill their various duties. But
of what value is the world when compared with the
value of the soul? This must be chiefly looked to, that
we perish not, that we run not upon an eternal undoing, and that our souls may live and it may be well with
us hereafter. We should first seek the kingdom of God
and then let other things be minded as they may. God
has never said, "First seek food and raiment and the
kingdom of heaven shall be added to you, righteousness shall be added, and salvation shall be added to
you"; but "Seek first the kingdom of God and His righteousness."

The same Holy Spirit who has said, "Be thou diligent to know the state of thy flocks, and look well to thy herds," Proverbs 27:23, has also said, "Only take heed to thyself and keep thy soul diligently," Deuteronomy 4:9; and, again, "Keep thy heart with all diligence (or above all keeping) for out of it are the issues of life," Proverbs 4:23. The question for the servants of God is, "How is it within? How goes on the work of mortification and sanctification?" Here they bestow their special labor in working out their salvation and in laying up treasures in heaven.

You should never count yourselves prosperous unless your souls are prospering. You should never count yourselves good husbandmen if your own vineyard has not been kept. You should never count yourselves wise servants unless you have been wise and busy for eternity.

The truly wise Christian does not take more business upon him than he can do without neglecting his soul. Though he employs himself, yet he does not entangle himself in the affairs of this life, "that he may please Him who hath chosen him to be a soldier," 2 Timothy 2:4.

This is the exhortation of our blessed Lord: "Take heed to yourselves, lest at any time your hearts be overcharged with surfeiting, and drunkenness, and cares of this life, and so that day come upon you unawares," Luke 21:34. The true Christian is willing to take the warning. He is wary how he undertakes more business than God calls him to. If God should put upon him a busier life and lay on a greater load of work or care upon him, he cheerfully undertakes it, knowing that, when God sets him to work, He will be with him in the work and help him out.

But, dear friends, are there not other masters who call you to work? It is not seldom that men's lusts call them to work. As their lusts call them off from work to waste time, to sleep, or to be idle, so frequently also men's lusts call them to work. Some men's pride calls them to work. Some men's prodigality calls them to work, that they may have something to spend on themselves or their companions. But most of all, perhaps, men's covetousness calls them to work. This is a hard and cruel master.

Oh, what a laborious, weary life such men live! Their life is a mere drudgery, rising early, going to bed late, eating the bread of carefulness. How many irons has the covetous man in the fire! How many schemes, plots, plans, and cares is he ever loaded with! He never rests; his hands are ever full; his thoughts are ever busy. Whatever he has done or gotten already, yet there is still more work coming in, more load laying on. This house or this other is to be gained or bought. This other pound or this other penny more is to be gathered; the ephah is not yet full. His greedy heart, that fountain of covetousness, is still crying out, "Get, get; gather, gather."

But, while you have been so busy here and there, what has been done for your souls? How does that work prosper? What trade has been driven for eternity? "Oh! I never thought of that. I had so many other things to do that I did not mind it."

Now a Christian thus resolves, "I will hear what God the Lord will speak. When God says, 'Go,' I will go. When he says 'Do this!' I will do it. I will have nothing to do of which I cannot say, 'This is that which the Lord would have to be done.' "

Thus, a Christian will look to the chief point, whatever may become of other matters. He will not engage further in any affairs than will be consistent with securing his great concernment—his everlasting interests. Whatever business he has, he must have time for his first duty. He must have his praying times, reading times, and hearing times. He must have his daily seasons for special converse with God, for communing with his own heart. He must duly set his watch and walk the rounds through his thoughts, affections, conscience, and all the powers of his soul; and, finding so much work, and of such great consequence, whatever else lacks, these must have his daily attendance.

While the poor worldling, who looks only to the things of this world, says, "I must have bread, riches, or increase of goods; I must not starve," the faithful Christian says, "I must have Christ. I must have grace, whether I have bread or not, or whether I starve or not. I must not walk the broad way to hell." A praying time is more necessary than an eating, drinking, or sleeping time and, therefore, much more necessary than a working time.

It is not the least part of a Christian's victory over the world to have, by the grace of God, the command of himself in lawful affairs and businesses. When he has such power over himself that he can assign to everything its proper place, measure, and season depending on the Lord, then he is conqueror.

Dear friends, how sadly does this speak concerning many of you? What say you, are you conquerors or captives? Let regard of your duty speak. Do not your oppressed and curtailed duties cry out, "We are beaten, we are beaten out of the field. We are not regarded when the world has any work to be done"? Guard against this for, believe it, when business gets the upper hand of duty, the world has gotten an advantage over the soul.

Is there not too great a fault among you on this account? Do not your businesses borrow from your duties, borrow but never pay? "Conscience, I pray you, excuse me from this praying time, from this hearing time, from this reading time. I pray, excuse me from this call upon the poor, the sick, the orphan, or the prisoner. I lack time to dispatch my business, hereafter I will pay it again."

How little of your time must ordinarily serve the turn for your attendance on God. A short prayer, perhaps, or short meditations are all you will allow; and your souls, ordinarily, fare accordingly. You are too much in haste to speed well. God will not bend His ear to vain, dead prayers.

If you have appointed your set times for prayer, do you keep your times? Does not the world ordinarily steal away your hours of prayer? When the time draws nigh for the worship of God, does not your corrupt heart step in, saying, "But I must be served first, my cattle must be served first, my customers must be served first. I have a friend that must be waited on first." Thus, when one business is dispatched, another falls in and another and another, till it is too late; and so all is put off till tomorrow, and when tomorrow comes, that day is as this day, and much busier.

Prayer is one of those weapons wherewith the battle is to be kept up against the world, Ephesians 6:18; Exodus 17:11. When the hands of Moses were lifted up, Amalek fell. And can you think the world has you not sure enough, when it can command your weapons out of your hands at its pleasure? Or, if it leaves them with you, can so blunt their edge that they are good for nothing? Is the world, then, made by you to give place to prayer, or is prayer made to give place to the world?

Never look to be other than worldlings while anything below has so much power with you as to hold you either under a total neglect or ordinary remissness in your religious duties. While it can keep you either so busy or so slothful that you refrain from prayer, it has you surely enough. If the devil can but keep you out of your closets, he will not fear to meet you in the field. He will not mind your standing on your feet if he can but keep you from falling on your knees.

Again, the victory which the children of God gain, by the grace of God, over the world consists in a power to use their worldly goods to their proper ends.

What is there which, when well used according to the will of God, will not bring a blessing with it? The Apostle Paul said, "We know that all things work together for good to them that love God," Romans 8:28. Then may we be truly said to enjoy what we have and to be secured from the mischiefs of it, when we have such power over it as to use it aright. He who has not a heart to use what he has, and use it well, is rather possessed *by* it than the possessor *of* it. Upon this account are worldly men the world's servants, servants of their estates rather than the masters of them. You cannot call him a master who is under the command of his servant, who cannot govern, nor order, nor dispose of himself and what he has but is always governed by it. The servant of the world will not eat, nor drink, nor give, nor spend but where the world gives him leave.

Who is a slave if he is a freeman?

He who, through faith, understands the power which he has over all that he possesses and the way to use it aright exercises his dominion accordingly; this man is lord and the world is his servant.

Now, God is the proper object to which all we have should be directed. God made all things for Himself; and He has put us in possession that we may use them for Him, for whom they are made. All the things which we have are talents entrusted in our hands by our Lord with this charge: "Occupy till I come," Luke 19:13. It will be but a poor account we shall give of what we have received if we bring not in every talent employed for God.

The faithful Christian will work for God, lay up for God, and lay out for God. He who works for bread or money and does not, therein, work for God, he who bestows anything upon his family for their present provision or their future portion and does not work for and bestow according to the will of God, and for the glory of God, is a wicked steward and unfaithful to his trust.

As we must work for God and bestow for God, so we must keep for God and save for God. A good steward must see there are no wastes made on his Lord's estate. He must not save anything from God; when God calls, he must keep nothing back from Him.

He should argue thus with himself: "There is a poor neighbor near who lacks bread. I will go and feed him. There is a poor orphan in want; I will go and take care of him. There is a company of poor children who are likely to be bred up in sin; I will go and be at charges with them, put them in school, or help to the disposing of them so that they may be bred up as Christians, in the nurture and admonition of the Lord."

He should save for God and see that there is no waste made, that nothing is spent upon his pride, upon his gluttonous appetite, upon his vain companions. He must not be prodigal of his estate to satisfy his own or other's lusts and humors. He must not be a niggard nor think to save anything from God. He who spends and he who saves from God will both prove but evil stewards. This saving will in the end prove the greatest wasting, as Christ says, "Whosoever will save his life shall lose it," Matthew 16:25. There is not a shorter way to want than by sinful parsimony: it is ill saving from God's poor. That bread which you save from the mouth of the poor, whom God would have you feed, that bread will become an eater. That which should have been given to God will eat out all your wealth.

Again, the victory which the children of God gain, by the grace of God, over the world consists in a power to despise the world's good things, to suffer the world's evil things, and to keep in the narrow way whether they prosper or suffer.

The Apostle thus wrote to the Philippians: "Not that I speak in respect of want: for I have learned, in whatsoever state I am, therewith to be content. I know both how to be abased, and I know how to abound: everywhere and in all things I am instructed both to be full and to be hungry, both to abound and to suffer need. I can do all things through Christ which strengtheneth me," Philippians 4:11-13.

To know how to want and how to abound is to know how to carry it as a Christian in both estates. Poverty and riches have each of them their tempta-

tions. The Apostle knew how to deal with either of
them, so that neither the one nor the other should
lead him away from duty, or draw him to anything unworthy of his Christian profession.

The Christian is not beholden to the world for his
religion (he has other arguments to persuade him to
be godly than that godliness is gain) and will not be
forced out of it by all that the world can give or take
away. As the loaves were not what drew him to Christ,
neither will the lack of bread drive him away. When
God is accepted as a sufficient portion so that we need
not the world to make us happy, when God is accounted our sure refuge so that we fear not that the
world can make us miserable, then it will be all one to
us whether the world is with us or against us.

Victory consists in contentment.

A true Christian knows that Christ is all and in all to
him, and that He is a sufficient reward and a sufficient
safeguard. He, thereupon, can be content in all his
wants and patient under all his sufferings.

He who can say, "God is my portion whether I want
or abound. I have never so much but I have need of
God; I have never so little but that I shall find God to
be all-sufficient," is he who can say, "God is my refuge
whether I am in safety or in danger. I am never in such
hazards but, in God, I am secure. I am never so out of
hazard but I need His security." How little is it that the
world, with all its glory on the one hand and all its fury
on the other, can do against that soul! Such a one
needs not the world to make him happy nor does he
fear that the world can make him miserable. He may

then go on his way rejoicing. He may serve the Lord without fear, in holiness and righteousness, all the days of his life.

He who knows what pinching lack and piercing sufferings are should understand that none but God can hold him up or bear him through, that in God alone he can find a supply for every want and a medicine for every wound. You are mistaken if you think that natural hardiness and self-confidence will do, without divine support, in trying cases.

God enables His saints, by His Spirit, to exercise self-denial under the greatest opportunities for self-indulgence and self-satisfaction. Self-denial, properly, is neglecting the interest and crossing the inclinations of the flesh in order to serve God.

He who might abound in wealth and yet, for Christ's sake and through faith in Him, is content to be in want; he who might live at ease or in honor and yet, for Christ's sake and through faith in Him, is content to be vile or dishonored; he who chooses to be holy rather than honorable and to be one of Christ's poor ones rather than one of the world's servants; he who, upon the account of Christ, flies from worldly advantages when these fly after him is the Christian indeed.

To neglect the world when the world neglects us or flies from us; not to seek great things for ourselves when we have no hope of obtaining them; not to be mindful of pleasing our pride or our appetite when we have not wherewith to maintain them; to fast when we have no bread and to put on sackcloth when we have no better raiment; not to contend for our will when we see we cannot have our will—there is nothing in all this. But voluntarily to lay down all at the feet of Christ, to part with all for the sake of Christ when we might have even what we would in a way of sin, is a great testimony how high the interest of Christ is exalted and how low the love of the world is brought in us.

One great instance of this self-denial you may read of: "By faith Moses, when he was come to years, refused to be called the son of Pharaoh's daughter; choosing rather to suffer affliction with the people of God, than to enjoy the pleasures of sin for a season," Hebrews 11:24-25.

Observe it—fairer opportunities for self-pleasing, for living in the splendor of worldly glory, and the grandeur of a prime favorite in the court of a king, few of the sons of men ever enjoyed. He was the adopted son of Pharaoh's daughter; and, upon this account, what his hopes and advantages might be, it is easy to imagine.

But, at once, he forsook all. He had a service to do for his God and such an affection for the people of God that immediately he put himself out of Pharaoh's favor and cast in his lot among his suffering brethren.

God enables His saints, by His Spirit, to exercise contentment under the greatest trials and difficulties.

Contentment is having the heart at ease, being well pleased with our condition without quarreling with our lot, without murmuring against God, and without self-tormenting vexations. Those whose god is the world cannot long be quiet. The world, like the moon, waxes and wanes; the world, like the sea, ebbs and flows; and so it is with the wicked. It is written, "But the wicked are like the troubled sea, when it cannot rest, whose waters cast up mire and dirt. There is no peace, saith my God, to the wicked," Isaiah 57:20-21.

What a poor and contemptible thing does the Bible show the world to be—a figure, a shadow, an image, a dream, vanity, a lie, things that are not, of no consistency or endurance.

My soul! go boldly forth,
Forsake this sinful earth:
What hath it been to thee,
But pain and sorrow:
And think'st thou it will be
Better tomorrow?

Love not the world's bright room,
Nor yet its gilded tomb,
Though on it written be
Man's grandeur-story:
Look up, by faith, and see
Sure, joyful glory.

Why art thou for delay?
Thou cam'st not here to stay.
What seek'st thou for thy part,
But heavenly pleasure?
Where, then, should be thy heart,
But where's thy treasure?

Thy God does reign above;
There is the world of love;
Mansions there purchas'd are,
By Christ's own merit:
For these He doth prepare
Saints by His Spirit.

O blessed company,
Where all in harmony,
Jehovah's praises sing,
Still, without ceasing:
And all obey their King
With perfect pleasing.

What joy must needs there be,
Where all God's glory see,
Feeling His vital love
Which still is burning;
And flaming heavenward move
Full love returning.

Look up to heaven, and see
How vast those regions be,
Where blessed spirits dwell,
How pure and lightful!
But earth is near to hell:
How dark and frightful!

Lord Jesus! take my spirit:
I trust Thy love and merit:
Take home Thy wandering sheep,
For Thou hast sought it:
My soul in safety keep,
For Thou hast bought it.

When the Word of God speaks of the world to
come, how highly does it speak of it! What a wonderful
and glorious report does it make of heaven, the state
of blessedness prepared for the saints! It is called a
kingdom, a crown, an eternal weight of glory, ad inheritance incorruptible, undefiled, that fades not away,
everlasting riches, rest, joy.

How awfully does it speak concerning hell, the state
of condemnation! It is called a prison, a place of dark-

ness, a bottomless pit, a lake of fire where there is weeping, wailing, and gnashing of teeth.

Oh, search the Scriptures and what these testify concerning the world! Believe the Scriptures, which have written vanity and vexation of spirit upon all under the sun. Understand what an insignificant nonentity this world is. Believe your own words; you can sometimes speak contemptibly of the world yourselves. You will acknowledge that the fashion of the world passes away. Do you think as you speak? Do not dissemble; either speak your minds plainly that this earth is your substance, your treasure, your portion and that it is worth venturing your souls for it, or that this is not your rest, that you have here no continuing city, that there is no building on this sand, that there is no contentment nor continuance here. If you go on to speak thus, believe your own words, and then judge how wisely you deal for yourselves in venturing your eternal happiness for such empty, perishing things.

The world is too little, when at its fullest, to fill the heart, to extend itself equal to man's expanding desires. What, then, is the world to content a man? When it has spent all its store, his cry will be, "What! no more? Is this all?"

God is the same and changes not, though the manifestations of God to the soul of man are not always the same. They are sometimes brighter and sometimes dimmer; sometimes He reveals Himself to the soul, and at other times He appears to withdraw. Hereupon, there is sometimes less quiet in the hearts of the saints than at other times; but while the heart feels that God is there, there is no lack. Disquiets there may be, but it is not whether the world waxes or wanes, ebbs or flows, but whether God is present or absent that makes the change upon the spirit of the saint. His language is, "Let God be with me, and then let the world be with whom it will. Let me have a houseful, or but a handful, it is all one as to my soul's contentment."

A true Christian is as little beholden to the world for his contentment as he is for his godliness. As he will be godly without asking permission of the world, so he will be contented whether the world will or not. Godliness and contentment both grow together. As much as you find of the one, so much of the other. If contentment is but small, godliness is not great; they grow both together, and the same root bears them both. Godliness comes down from heaven, and never did contentment spring up out of the earth. They have the same origin; both come from God.

They who give way to discontent should look to it that they are not strangers from God. How can they consider that they belong to God who need so much of the world to keep them in peace? If the world is that which alone can content them, then it will be still their god. Oh, what restless spirits some men have; never well, never at rest! What is the matter? What is there lacking? What quiet are they seeking for? Is it for a better house, a greater estate; better trading, greater ease or greater honor as their rest and peace? Must they be rich, must they have all to their minds, or will they still be thus discontented? If this is the case, they must serve the world then. If they cannot find contentment for their souls in God, they shall find no other portion than that of this world.

If the world can content you, be sure it can command you. If you make it your paymaster, it will be your taskmaster.

Where will men not go, what will they not do for contentment! Why do they run so often from God but for their contentment? What do men seek in their fields, in their shops, in their palaces, in their cottages, among their companions, but their contentment? That is, company to please, wealth for their indulgence, honor to gratify them and pleasure to content their minds.

They mistake the matter. Contentment does not grow in any of these fields. It no more dwells in palaces than in cottages; yet men will think no labor too great for anything that promises them contentment. This the world promises: "I will content you; I will content you." As long as men take its word, it has them sure enough for servants. At once, find your mistake. Hear riches say, "Contentment is not in me." Hear pleasure saying, "It is not in me." Hear friends saying, "It is not in us." Then you may judge how the world has no power to content you.

At once, hear every creature and every condition telling you, "It is not in me to content you. It is from above that your contentment must come." Then, when you see that all the world cannot content you, the lack of the world need not discontent you.

Contentment in God will be one of the best evidences of your conquest over the world. He is a Christian of proof who cannot be contented with the world, and yet can be contented without it; who cannot be contented with the world when he has most of it, and yet can be content when he has the least of it.

Oh, what a constant calm and serenity should we feel in our spirits, what steadiness would appear in our lives, and what triumph over the world and all its changes should we possess if once we embraced this truth in our hearts that in God alone our contentment lies!

Oh, how much below the excellency and the sweetness of such a life do we live! How hard are we to be pleased! How soon out of patience! What a small matter will disturb and distract our hearts!

When distress approaches, when the Lord frowns upon us and keeps us low and short of what our minds desire, then how few of us can say, "It is well!"

Dear friends, look not on discontent as a little evil. Think not that it is a trifling sin to count it but a small thing for God to save our souls unless He will please our tastes, to count it but a small thing that God should give us our lives unless He also gives us our wills; as if nothing would please us, unless the Lord will set us on the throne and let us live for ourselves and to our satisfaction in this world.

God enables His saints, by His Spirit, to exercise humility when they are in the height of honor.

Some saints have been highly exalted in the world, have been raised from the dust to sit with the princes among the people and have been numbered among the great and the honorable. Thus, Abraham was exalted. Thus, Joseph, raised from a prison, was lifted up to be the second in the kingdom. Mordecai was exalted from the threshold of the king's house to be the man whom the king delighted to honor. David was exalted from the sheepfold to the throne.

Others have known great renown for their noble acts and mighty works which they have done. How was it with David upon his slaughter of the Philistine, with

Daniel upon his interpretation of the king's dream, and with the Apostles upon the miracles that they wrought?

These holy men looked up to God as their Father and their King. They bowed before His majesty and abased themselves before Him. The language of their hearts was the same as that of Abraham who, speaking to the Lord, said that he was but dust and ashes, Genesis 18:27.

Those who, by the grace of God, can keep humble in such heights, whose hearts still keep their dwelling on the lower ground; who are little ones in all their greatness—little in their own eyes and willing to be little in the eyes of others; who can take the crowns which are set on their heads and lay them down before the Lord; who count it their honor to decrease that He may increase—these are the persons whose humility is of the true stamp.

A tempting world will say to saint as well as sinner, "Do you not know yourself who you are, what you have, and how you are esteemed? Everyone loves you, admires you, applauds and speaks well of you, and you have merit enough in you to deserve it all! Why should you not accept all this respect and be of the same mind with all who know you? Why should you not think as well of yourself, prize your own worth, and know your own place, as well as they?"

Then, it is nobler in saints to have all checked and repelled with such thoughts as these: "But who am I that I should lift myself up? What have I that I have not received? I have wisdom, I have talents, I have riches, but whose are all these? Are they my own? Are they of my own procuring? If I have done anything for God, through whose strength was it that I was enabled to do it? In whose name was it? It was by the strength and in the name of the Lord, to Him be all the glory."

Peter and John had performed a great cure upon the lame man, and the people were greatly taken with it. They ran together to see these Apostles and wondered at them on account of the cure which they had wrought. But the Apostles were not at all transported with the people's astonishment and would not accept their applause. They said, "Ye men of Israel, why marvel ye at this? or why look ye so earnestly on us, as though by our own power or holiness we had made this man to walk? The God of Abraham, and of Isaac, and of Jacob, the God of our fathers, hath glorified his Son Jesus; whom ye delivered up, and denied him in the presence of Pilate, when he was determined to let him go. But ye denied the Holy One and the Just, and desired a murderer to be granted unto you; and killed the Prince of life, whom God hath raised from the dead; whereof we are witnesses. And His name, through faith in His name, hath made this man strong, whom ye see and know: yea, the faith which is by Him hath given him this perfect soundness in the presence of you all," Acts 3:12-16.

Victory consists in magnanimity.

God enables His saints, by His Spirit, to exercise magnanimity amidst the greatest difficulties and dangers.

In magnanimity there are these two great principles: generosity and fortitude.

The newborn soul is generous. Renewed as it is by

the Spirit of God, it is bent upon doing mighty works for God and will not be satisfied to do some merely little or low things. The worldly spirit is a poor and narrow spirit, inhabiting sluggish, dull, and heavy souls for whom either a little action must suffice or, if there is more, it is about little things. The world-conquering soul is a soul upon the wing that, bursting the fetters of earth, flies high and pursues higher things by a swift and most vigorous motion. God has done great things for it, and this great soul is bent upon rendering great obedience to the Lord.

Such a soul seeks great things, and it dares to attempt great things. It will not despond or be discouraged at difficulties saying "This is too much" or "This is too hard." Difficulties are the trial and the proof of a generous soul.

They who are children of God must fight their way. They must carry on the battle against corruptions within, against temptations, and against the powers of darkness without, and this is the fight of faith. The weapons of the saints' warfare are not carnal but mighty, through God, to the pulling down of strongholds. Though they walk in the flesh, they do not war after the flesh, 2 Corinthians 10:3-4. Eternal life is the crown set before them by the Lord, for their encouragement in their good warfare. This crown they must lay hold on, as those who are afraid of coming short of it and losing it: "Hold that fast which thou hast, that no man take thy crown," Revelation 3:11.

"What," asks the faithful Christian, "shall I do for God, whom my soul loves and honors? What shall I *not* do? What shall I refuse to hazard for His sake? Oh, what little things are my great things, even the greatest that I can do! How much I have received; how little I have returned! Oh, for more zeal in the work for God, for more strength for work! I can never do enough when I have done all and, therefore, I will never say it is enough while there is more to be done."

But, how little will suffice a worldly soul, and how much is every little accounted! A generous soul does much and then thinks all but little; a worldly soul does little but over reckons that little. A little praying, or praising, or speaking, or thinking must serve, and how that little is made much of!

How soon are such men at their work's end and have even wrought themselves out of work, or else how quickly are they discouraged by the greatness of their work. The least straw is a stumbling block, the least molehill is a mountain; every duty is a difficulty, and every difficulty is an impossibility!

Oh, dear friends, where are the victorious spirits? Where are the heroes of Christianity, the nobles who have set their necks to the yoke in the work of the Lord? What designs have you for advancing in holiness, for magnifying the grace of God in you, for exalting His name in a heavenly life? Where are the trophies of your prowess? Bring forth the prisoners which you have taken. Can you show your lusts, your pride, and your covetousness in chains? Can you show the prisoners which you have taken—houses, honors, dignities, pleasures, with your feet upon the necks of them all?

This should be the feeling and expression of our hearts: "The weight is laid aside, and now we will run with patience the race which is set before us. Now for a fruitful life, for laboring and abounding in the work of the Lord, for growing rich unto God and rich in good works. We cannot sit down by that little which we have done. The Lord is worthy; He is worthy for whom we should do other manner of things than these, for whom we should live another manner of life than this." Oh, were we all soul, all wing, all life, all action, how little would our all be to what we wish it were!

Read in the Book of God and search what the Lord has done for man—how He has offered to pardon, to sanctify, and to redeem man out of the house of bondage—and then ask, "What honor has been done to the Lord, what gratitude has been shown to Him for all this?" And think how apt you are to hang back from the work of the Lord, to lessen your time for prayer, to keep apart from the public worship of God, to withhold your hand from helping the sick, the needy, and prisoners, to neglect confessing Christ and declaring to all around the truths of His gospel.

With cold lips, and colder hearts, men call the Savior blessed while they do not seek to partake of His blessedness. They call Him holy while they do not seek to be partakers of His holiness. Ah! Is it of Him, so kind, so merciful, so bountiful, so glorious, that they should talk thus coldly? The Apostles and holy men of old, in the spirit and power of a gracious, saving knowledge, spoke of His unsearchable riches and the exceeding preciousness of His love shown forth in His vicarious sufferings and death, with burning hearts and lips as touched by a live coal from off the altar. Their souls were fired by the love of God. No wonder, then, that their preaching and exhortations ran with electric force and power through the hearts of their hearers.

Oh, that we had many, many such confessors of

Christ among us now, many whose delight and glory-
ing it would be to proclaim to the ends of the earth the
mercy, lovingkindness, and love of God shown forth to
a guilty world in the gift of His own dear Son, Jesus
Christ!

In fortitude, the faithful Christian stands against
the fury of the world. That is a magnanimous spirit
which delights in difficulties and despises danger, and
a bold soul that not only loves to serve but dares to suffer, that is not careful about the threatenings of perse-
cutors, Daniel 3:16; that none of all these things move,
Acts 20:24, and that is strong and of good courage.

Christian Fortitude.

Christian fortitude consists in:
1. A boldness with God.
2. A boldness in God.
3. A boldness for God.

1. Christian fortitude consists in a boldness with
God, in which is included a free and confident access
to God, coming boldly unto the throne of grace, Hebrews 4:16. This boldness arises from a sense of reconciliation with God, through faith in Christ, from an
inward acquaintance with God from a conscience of
uprightness before the Lord. The Apostle thus wrote to
the Hebrews, "Having, therefore, brethren, boldness to
enter into the holiest by the blood of Jesus, by a new
and living way, which He hath consecrated for us,
through the veil, that is to say, His flesh; and having a
high priest over the house of God, let us draw near
with a true heart in full assurance of faith, having our

hearts sprinkled from an evil conscience, and our bodies washed with pure water," Hebrews 10:19-22.

There is no coming before God with boldness while the heart is guileful and cleaves to its beloved sin. It is being without guile that gives boldness. It is the hypocrite who is afraid and ashamed to appear before God. He goes into his closet, or into the place of worship, to shuffle over in haste his poor form of words and is glad to be away again. He prays no proper prayer; he is not free or open-hearted with God; a sense of his determination to cleave to sin stops his mouth.

Dear friends, you who think you shall be bold for the Lord, who now have a forward mind to own the worship and ways of God and have hope that in nothing you shall be ashamed, but that, at all times and in all things, Christ shall be magnified in you whether by life or by death, whenever you are put to the trial, let us ask you, "Do you have boldness with God? Is He your Friend? Is it peace between Him and your souls?"

Time was when there was no peace. Have you now peace with God? You were runaways and rebels against God. Your natural state was a state of enmity. Are you reconciled by the blood of Christ? Have you returned and become converts to God? It is folly to talk of being bold with God until you are brought home unto God. This is as if the stubble would be bold with the flames. It is to dash on the rock, to sleep on the waves, to take sanctuary in wrath and fury, and to trust in indignation; as little succor and relief will the unconverted find from the Lord. Are you reconciled? Are you the friends of God?

Are you acquainted with God? Friends may grow

strangers, and strangers cannot be bold. Are you used
to conversing and walking with God? How often do you
seek His favor and presence? Is there constant inter-
course and correspondence maintained between the
Lord and your souls?

Are you tender how you break your peace and lose
your acquaintance with God? Is it your care to walk before Him in uprightness? Do you not ordinarily grieve,
or offend, or carelessly neglect the Lord? Is there no
allowed treachery or falsehood in your hearts to Him?
Is every sin against God a wound to your own souls?
Are you ever angry with yourselves other than when
God is at peace with you? Is it your constant care to
"have always a conscience void of offence toward God
and toward men," Acts 24:16; and, hereupon, can you
come boldly before the throne of grace and make
known your wants and your grievances and ease your
hearts by opening them to the Lord? Fear not, your
boldness with the Lord will give you boldness on behalf
of God, however frightful the case may be.

Only let us tell you (for fear of discouraging such
who should not be discouraged), he who has the
ground of this holy boldness; who, through the blood
of Jesus, has peace with God; whose constant care it is
to please the Lord and to walk before Him in uprightness (though, by reason of the darkness and misgivings
of his troubled, trembling heart, he scarce dares to call
God Father, can hardly at any time look Him in the
face without fear and shame and, hereupon, shakes at
the forethought of the day of trial); this poor, trembling soul may expect, when he is put to it, to be enabled to stand as Mount Zion that shall never be removed.

2. Christian fortitude consists in a boldness in God. "We were bold in our God," says the Apostle, 1 Thessalonians 2:2. This boldness stands in a firm dependence upon God: "Though He slay me, yet will I trust in Him," Job 13:15.

The Psalmist, addressing God, said, "Thou shalt guide me with Thy counsel," Psalm 73:24. The faithful Christian will not lean to his own understanding. He is fearful to walk in his own counsels. He knows that it is not in man who walks to direct his own steps, but withal he knows he has a better guide. He depends on God for His aid and assistance. He holds in faith the same principle and assurance which is expressed in these words of our Lord Jesus Christ Himself: "For the Lord God will help me; therefore shall I not be confounded: therefore have I set my face like a flint, and I know that I shall not be ashamed. He is near that justifieth me; who will contend with me? let us stand together: who is mine adversary? let him come near to me. Behold, the Lord God will help me; who is he that shall condemn me? lo, they all shall wax old as a garment; the moth shall eat them up," Isaiah 50:7-9.

That God will provide, protect, and strengthen is the comfort and encouragement of the faithful Christian in the most difficult cases. Hence, he bears up under the most awful aspects of his present case, whatever it may be. Thus, David encouraged himself in the Lord his God, 1 Samuel 30:6. Thus, the Apostle Paul encouraged his brethren in Christ, 1 Corinthians 10:13. The faithful Christian, under all his trials and distresses, can say with the Psalmist, "Why art thou cast down, O my soul? and why art thou disquieted within me? Hope in God: for I shall yet praise Him, who is the health of my countenance, and my God," Psalm 43:5.

3. Christian fortitude consists in a boldness for God. Boldness for God is shown in a constant maintaining our fidelity and allegiance to God, in a resolved promoting of the interest and honor of His name and worship. It is a boldness to pray, as in the case of Daniel, though the king forbade him, Daniel 6:10; a boldness to preach, as in the case of the Apostles, though the priests and rulers forbade them, Acts 5:40-42; a boldness to be holy and upright and not sin against God, as in the case of Job, though the devil afflicted him for it, Job 1:22; a boldness to confess Christ before men in all seasons, and under all circumstances, bearing witness both by words and works against all the sins, the profaneness, the atheism, the idolatries, and the apostasies of the world; a boldness to suffer rather than to sin.

When men, influenced by faith in Christ, follow God and keep His way, making light of the greatest advantages, on the one hand, and the sharpest sufferings, on the other; when the highest price that the world can give cannot entice them, and the greatest persecution which the world can inflict cannot force them to unfaithfulness; when its best and its worst are despised in comparison to a good conscience towards God, then a noble victory is gained over the world.

You would be, perhaps, afraid to commit some horrid sins, such as to blaspheme the name of God, to cast off the profession of religion, to apostatize from it, or to openly renounce Christ. These horrid wickednesses have too ghastly a face, these look too much to belong to hell; you dare not, perhaps, buy your liberty or your life at so dear a rate. But if you think that you will gain happiness or security by some little sin, by some little compliance, or by that which has but the appearance of evil, what do you say now? If you cannot drink down a full draft of the cup of iniquity, can you not sip of the cup, put it to your mouth, or even kiss the cup? Ah! You ought to know that every drop is poison. Every little sin is the price of blood. Even the very appearance of evil will be a blot on your holy profession.

Boldness for God is a humble boldness. It does not make a mere noise. It does not boast and bluster, nor show itself in uncomely heats and animosities. It has firmness and undauntedness, but these are joined with lowliness and meekness.

Boldness for God is a prudent boldness. It does not take up needless controversies. It is cautious of mistaking matters or measures. It does not rashly and heedlessly run upon dangers which it might without sin avoid. It does not unwarily make enemies nor needlessly provoke them but, if men will be enemies, it fears not to meet them in its way and will neither turn aside nor stand still to escape them.

Now, put all these together. He who is bold with the Lord, being reconciled by the blood of Christ and walking before Him in his integrity, can, with a holy courage, approach and make known his requests to the Lord for grace, mercy, and help in the time of need. He who is bold in the Lord has his heart fixed, trusting in God. He who is bold for the Lord is faithful to God; is holy and righteous; will follow God and keep His way with the neglect of the highest worldly advantages, on the one hand, and the sharpest sufferings on the other; will choose the greatest sufferings rather than commit even little sins; will refuse the greatest advantages rather than neglect the least duties; is meek, and yet mighty through God; trembles at the Word, and yet stands out against the world; is tender as a bruised reed, and yet not terrified at an army with banners; is whom a child may lead, and yet a giant cannot drive; is a harmless dove with a serpent's wisdom and a patient lamb with a lion's heart; will submit to insult and injury and yet, in the strength of the Lord, will contend against the world, the flesh, and the devil. This is the valiant Christian who triumphs indeed. In the name of Christ, he has spoiled principalities and powers.

Dear Christian friends, depend upon the Lord in all holy boldness. "Be strong in the grace that is in Christ Jesus, endure hardness as a good soldier of Jesus Christ," 2 Timothy 2:1,3.

In whom, then, can we find this mighty spirit of Christianity? Behold, some who seem sufficiently high-flown are yet as weak as water—whose hopes and whose comforts lie exposed to a variety of temptations; whose religion will strike its colors at the sight of every enemy; who are nobody but in the sunshine and the calm; whose course must be steered by their interest and safety; who speak of being faithful, yet keep back their hearts from God; who protest against iniquity, yet will sin rather than suffer!

Oh, beware, you who make your formal prayers to serve instead of a heartfelt and sincere turning to God —your outward forwardness in the cause of God to serve, instead of heartily accepting the grace of God. He needs not, nor will He regard, your smooth words while you are His enemies. He will not accept the worship of your lips while your hearts are far from Him. Be reconciled to God, accept His grace, resign yourselves to Him, accept Him as Lord and Ruler over you, let His law and His love be in your hearts; and then you may be bold, both upon His acceptance of whatever service you do for His name and upon your security in it. Be the Lord's in truth, and then fear not to make the Lord your trust.

Victory consists in a steady mind despite outward changes.

God enables His saints to maintain an equal, steady, fixed frame of mind, in all the changes of their outward condition. He is a Christian, indeed, who is established in faith, believing in Christ, depending on His righteousness. His soul is not deprived of its peace; his feet are not turned out of their course by all the tossings and changes of his outward state; his heart is not moved within, though every day should prove that all he has without is movable. Both in his prosperity and in his patience, he possesses his soul. He still goes on in the service of God and in resistance against the devil. He is still traveling on heavenward and turns away from the world which lies in iniquity.

Whatever changes pass over the wicked, their hearts, mainly, are not changed. They are ever beside themselves and yet ever themselves. They are wicked still, ungodly still, hardened still, for sin and the devil still. Let their condition be what it will—let them be in health, let them be sick, let their way be strewn with roses or hedged with thorns, let them be joyful, let them be sad—all is one. They are the same men and holding the same course. They are wicked under mercies, wicked under judgments, wicked in their joys, wicked in their sorrows.

With regard to the saints of God, let the world do what it can against them. Let it shine or thunder upon them, deal gently or deal roughly, feed or famish them, they are still where they were. Their heart is fixed, trusting in God.

To show the different characters of the saints and of the wicked, we will turn to the words of God's awful curse, "Thus saith the Lord, Cursed be the man that trusteth in man, and maketh flesh his arm, and whose heart departeth from the Lord. For he shall be like the heath in the desert, and shall not see when good cometh; but shall inhabit the parched places in the wilderness, in a salt land and not inhabited," Jeremiah 17:5-6; and now to the words of God's blessing, "Blessed is the man that trusteth in the Lord, and whose hope the Lord is. For he shall be as a tree planted by the waters, and that spreadeth out her roots by the river, and shall not see when heat cometh, but her leaf shall be green; and shall not be careful in the year of drought, neither shall cease from yielding fruit," Jeremiah 17:7-8.

Consider, dear friends, it may be that while the Lord has prospered you and outward matters have gone according to your wishes, then you could love, serve, praise, and rejoice in the Lord. Then you could be active, lively, and faithful and cheerfully go on your way. But the first cross which you have met with has been as water poured on all your fire. A little storm that has risen has put out much of your light, turned you aside from duties and comforts, turned you from praying and rejoicing in God to vexing, fretting, and murmuring against His ways. How one frosty night withers away all the flowers that your sunshine has nursed up!

Or else, if your souls have been much prospering in the winter, how the next summer has choked them up with weeds! Sometimes when God has proved you in the furnace of affliction, how humble, serious, and mortified you have been! Then what praying, repenting, and covenanting with God; then how you have sought to be dead to sin, crucified to the world, to live by faith, and to walk in fear. Nothing but God, holiness and glory would then satisfy your desires; but no sooner has He brought you out of darkness into light and redeemed your soul out of trouble, but all is presently forgotten, and worldliness, vanity, and careless security return upon you.

Oh, how little is there yet done to what should be done, ere you shall come to any steadiness, while every worldly change distracts and disorders you!

Seek earnestly after a more abundant gift of that grace which alone can establish, strengthen, settle you. Let the Psalmist's prayer to God be yours: "Uphold me with Thy free Spirit," Psalm 51:12.

Have you received of the gifts of the Holy Spirit? Have you a little grace? Seek for more; pray for a double portion of the Spirit.

Our Heavenly Father has promised to give His Spirit to those who ask Him. The reason why we go on from day to day with so little grace is because our little suffices us. We are content and sit down satisfied with that little. They who dwell at the throne of grace, whose very breath is prayer, who are constantly and anxiously seeking for God's blessing, whom one blessing will not suffice but are still seeking for more and more, these are the thriving souls, full of faith and full of the Spirit.

Oh, be aspiring Christians! Look up to the highest and do not be content to take up with low attainments. Follow on to know, to serve, to imitate the Lord and Savior, Jesus Christ!

Let your hearts be more firmly fixed upon God. The more faithfully that God is regarded, the less impression will any worldly things make upon your hearts. When the soul exerts all its powers in the vigorous pursuit of the invisible crown; when the heart is possessed and taken up with its more weighty and glorious concernments; when the thoughts, affections, and resolutions are all deeply engaged and busily bent towards God, the greatest occurrences of this life are passed over as little things. It is because you are so indolent and indifferent in going heavenward that you are so moved by every trifle.

Let the importance of your eternal state be much in view and deeply impressed upon your hearts. Look often into the blessed eternity that is before you. Be much and often in the contemplation of the heavenly world, and when your hearts are raised and warmed into admirings of the glory, then ask what little things are the sunshine or the storms of this lower world. You may then say, "Tell me not of crosses or disappointments here; but how I shall get to heaven! If I may but arrive there, it is of little moment what befalls me here."

Do not allow yourselves what merely pleases self; opportunities are often only temptations. Accustom yourselves to wish for no more than God allows to you, and you shall find that God will never give less than will content you. He who, whatever happens, whatever his portion or condition may be, in every turn or change that comes, can find his heart still saying, "It is with me as it should be"; he whose heart says of every condition he is in, "It is well"—that man has obtained an important conquest over the world.

Victory consists in a willingness to die.

Victory over the world consists also in a willingness to leave this world and take our flight to heaven. It consists in a willingness to die.

Worldly men, if they could help it, would never die. They would rather live among the dead than die into a better life. They are dead while they are alive, dead in sin, and they wish that this might be their eternal state. If they might be allowed an eternal day to sin in, what other heaven would they wish for? Were there a message brought to the vain world that their houses of clay should stand forever; that their buying, selling, building, planting, getting wealth, and rolling themselves in pleasures should be their everlasting employment; that all the noise and fear of suffering, sickness, and death should be forever silenced, what a grateful message, what good news, would this be to them!

Death is the great dread of the world, the king of terrors, Job 18:14. The hope of heaven would willingly be parted with so that the fear of death might be no more. How the expectation and approach of death appalls the faces, weakens the hands, shakes the hearts, sours the pleasures, dampens the gaieties, and alarms the spirits of the worldly ones of the earth!

If it should be said this day to any of you who are still worldlings, "Set your house in order, for you shall die and not live"; if you should see written on your walls "Your day is finished, this night shall your soul be required of you. You have eaten your last morsel, drunk your last draft, and your last sand is running out"; were this the message to you this day, what a sad funeral sermon would it be to you! But the faithful saint is ready to be gone out of this world.

Good old Simeon said, "Lord, now lettest Thou Thy servant depart in peace, according to Thy Word: for mine eyes have seen Thy salvation," Luke 2:29-30. The Apostle Paul said, "I am in a strait betwixt two, having a desire to depart, and to be with Christ which is far better," Philippians 1:23. Thus, then, may the saint say, "Go forth, O my soul, do not linger. You have served the Lord Christ; fear not, therefore, in His strength and through His intercession and atonement, to go forth and receive your inheritance."

You who seek to triumph over death upon good grounds have said unto it, in the words of the Apostle, "O death, where is thy sting? O grave, where is thy victory?" Yet, when it comes in earnest, you do not know how the flesh may shrink. But yet, if it does, be not discouraged.

It will be your wisdom to meet your dying day as the most joyful day of your life; to buckle on all your armor, all your hopes, all your graces, all your evidences, all your experiences and comforts; and to expect that the conflict of that day may be such as to need your utmost preparations for it.

Worldly men are unwilling to meet death because it deprives them of all their treasures. That which they have they cannot carry with them, and they are unwilling to leave it behind. They cannot carry their money, their houses, or their lands with them. They covet, they purchase, they build, and they lay up with as much care and zeal as if they could carry with them all they have into the other world; yet, as they came in naked, so they must go naked out of this world, Job 1:21.

As this is a certain truth—that man, as long as he is selfish and earthly-minded, must be destitute of true life, the life of the Holy Spirit, in his soul—what, then, should be more dreaded than a way of worldly ease and prosperity! What a misery, nay, what a curse, is there in everything which gratifies and nourishes our self-love and self-esteem. As man, in his natural state, lies in this darkness, how anxiously should he seek new light and a new life in Jesus Christ, in whom alone these can be found!

To the Christian who has conquered the world, the world from thenceforth ceases to be his treasure. What a worldling has here is his treasure, for it is all he has. Christ is a treasure, but He is not his; heaven is a treasure, but it is not his. This earth is all that he has.

Those who indulge themselves in the gifts and pleasures of the world and are sunk and drowned in earthly-mindedness only deceive themselves and others when they say they are willing to die. Do you say, "If I were sure that Christ were mine, I would not care to live a day longer. I lack assurance, and that is the reason why I would yet wish to abide longer in this tabernacle"? No, no, there is something more in the matter. The world has still such a hold of your affections. The pleasures you find in an earthly life—your friends, your goods, and the contentment you have therein—have

so taken a hold on you that you cannot yet find it in
your heart to part with them. Search narrowly and see
if you do not find the matter to be thus with you. You
can never expect to be more willing to die till you find
your heart more loose from the pleasures and satisfac-
tions of an earthly life.

He is the true Christian whose soul is already dead
to the world, who is ready to depart out of life. Those
who live in communion with God; whose souls are
weaned from the world; who, through a self-denying
course, find the pleasures of their senses lose their
gratefulness to them; who converse with eternity and
delightful previews of the happiness above, and who
have already carried up to heavenly enjoyments; these
are the Christians who are ready to depart out of life.
We will believe such a one, that he is in earnest, when
he can truly say with the Apostle, "For to me to live is
Christ, and to die is gain," Philippians 1:21.

Worldly men are also unwilling to die because of an
uncertainty as to where they shall go when they depart
hence, and what world they shall find when they leave
this world. Upon this ground, we cannot wonder that
worldlings are afraid to die. They may well indeed be
so, for death can only lead them into everlasting
abodes of misery. Captives to the world are captives to
the devil, and where will the devil carry his prisoners?

Who would be willing to leave his country, his habitation, and his acquaintance for an unknown land, especially when he had a fear that he should be sold as a
bondman? Such is your case, worldlings; and, therefore, it is no wonder that you think it is better to abide
here.

A Christian may know where he is going when he

goes hence. The Apostle Paul wrote thus to the Corinthians, "We know that if our earthly house of this tabernacle were dissolved, we have a building of God, a house not made with hands, eternal in the heavens. For in this we groan, earnestly desiring to be clothed upon with our house which is from heaven," 2 Corinthians 5:1-2. Whatever the dwelling of the Christian may be here, he is confident that he shall have one infinitely better when this fails. He groans, not under the ruin of this building, but in hope of a better building—even a house not made with hands, eternal in the heavens—earnestly desiring the day of a joyful resurrection.

It is true that a Christian, through the weakness of his faith, may not fully experience this confidence and, therefore, also, may fear to leave this world; yet he much prefers a life with God, in perfect holiness and blessedness, above the most prosperous worldly life. Though his flesh could wish a longer stay, yet his spirit is willing, whenever the Lord calls, to depart. According as the mortification of his flesh, his crucifixion to the world, and his assurance of salvation grow more complete and clear, so is his willingness heightened into more earnest desires and longings. He will then use such words as these: "Come, Lord Jesus, come quickly."

But you who are faithful Christians, whatever executioner is sent to take away your life—if it is old age, if a fever or consumption, if a fall, a fire, or any other casualty, if it is a son of violence or a murderer—whatever executioner is sent to take away your life and whether he comes in the first, second, or third watch, seek and pray that you may be able to use such lan-

guage as this of the Apostle Paul: "For I am now ready
to be offered, and the time of my departure is at hand.
I have fought a good fight, I have finished my course, I
have kept the faith; henceforth there is laid up for me
a crown of righteousness. which the Lord, the righteous Judge, shall give me at that day; and not to me
only, but unto all them also that love His appearing," 2
Timothy 4:6-8.

Every captive to the world is an unbeliever, is without Christ, and is in a state of condemnation. Oh,
think not lightly of your worldliness! It is a death-token
upon you, and it marks you as companions with those
who perish. That this is certainly so, that every worldling is an unbeliever and unconverted, we shall endeavor to make evident to you.

Can that man be a believer who is a lover of the
world more than a lover of God? Can you say that you
love God when your heart is with the world? Will this
be accepted when you bring to the Lord only a divided
heart? Speak, conscience, will God accept such a gift?
These are our Lord's own words: "He that loveth father
or mother more than Me is not worthy of Me; and he
that loveth son or daughter more than Me is not worthy of Me. And he that taketh not his cross, and fol-
loweth after Me, is not worthy of Me," Matthew 10:37-
38. Find, if you can, a more convincing characteriza-
tion of unbelievers than this: "Lovers of pleasures more
than lovers of God," 2 Timothy 3:4.

He who loves the world more than God is none of
His. And are you not the men? Do you love God as you
love the world? Let your lives speak: what do you seek?
Whom do you love? To whom do you yield yourselves
servants to obey? What is the chief pleasure and com-

fort of your lives? Do you rejoice in God, or is not the world the god whom you serve? Do you not seek to be rich and to prosper in the world more than you ever seek to be holy and righteous before God?

Love feels no load. Obedience is only painful to him who does not have the love of God in his heart.

He cannot be a true Christian who has not come to Christ. Coming to Christ and believing in Christ are the same. Do not deceive yourselves, you may as well be at the same time in heaven and hell as your hearts be with Christ and in the world.

The renouncing of the world is included in coming to Christ. Christ, when He says to men, "Come," says also, "Depart." And coming to Christ is, in the very nature of it, departing from the world; and choosing Him is a refusing of it. When Christ and the world are offered to you, can you choose both Christ and the world? Surely not.

Is your appetite for more of the world as greedy and insatiable as ever? Is your love, delight, and rest in what you have as great as ever? Is it so hard to get anything from you for the poor and needy, so that the little which comes is as the dropping of blood from your hearts? Are you so pinching and sparing that scarce any but your own selves are ever the better for you? Then have you yet renounced the world? Are you so vexed and tormented when you are crossed or disappointed in any little of your worldly interests? Then, how can you say you are crucified to the world? Do you keep back from public worship, prayer, sabbaths, sermons, and sacraments? Then how are you dead to the world? Has the world held you in such ignorance and atheism that, under all the means of knowledge and grace, you still live without God in the world without a saving knowledge of, or an interest in, Christ? Then how can you say that you have shaken off its yoke?

Thus, half-reformation ends in certain ruin. It is necessary to be thoroughly reformed and to give up all idols. The new creation is a whole and entire work. It consists in a complete change of heart. Through it, the children of the devil become the children of God. You have to deal with God, the Maker and the Searcher of hearts, and He will have nothing unless He has the heart; and none of that either, unless He has it all.

Would you pass over into His Kingdom and become His subjects? Then you must serve Him as your only Sovereign. Loyalty can admit of no rivalry. If Christ is your King, then His laws and scepter must rule all within you. You must acknowledge no foreign power; that would be treason. Your only safety is to make a heap of all worldly lusts and sinful affections and to have all sacrificed together, to live to no sin but altogether and only to God.

Thief! Cheat! Defrauder! When will you be honest?

"When my interest will give me leave."

Drunkard! When will you be sober?

"When my companions will give me leave."

Worldling! When will you give up all for Christ?

"When the world will give me leave."

Profligate! When will you be heavenly-minded?

"When my sensuality will give me leave."

How much of Christianity will you take up?

"What the world will allow me."

But, when will you get to heaven then?

"Why, when the flesh and the world are all agreed to send me there."

These are essentially the answers of sinners.

Learn and consider, O worldlings, that if ever you would get victory over the world, you must first possess another spirit. In vain do you think to live other than a worldly life while the spirit of the world lives in you. Have you been so long professors of Christianity and have not yet gotten the Spirit of Christianity? It is not the Spirit of Christ who leads you on in an earthly course! God does not give His Spirit to teach men how to be such drudges to the world. God does not give His Spirit to teach men how to follow the world and to make a treasure-heap of its riches, honors, and vanities.

What are the earth's riches, her designs, her courses, her ordinary talk and discourse? What are these but earth? But these are not the thoughts, the ways, and the language of the Spirit. Can anyone who beholds your conversation—which, in the general bent and tenor of it, is about the world with, perhaps, but now and then a cold wish or a few heartless words about the things of God—can any man who beholds you say, "These are the persons who are dead to the world, who are crucified, who are mortified to things below. These are they who have received the Spirit of Christ, indeed. These speak like Christians, look like Christians, and live like Christians, like men of another world"?

Can it be said thus of you, that your course is a spiritual course, that your lives are spiritual lives, and that your steps are all bending to a heavenly country? Would not your daily course and your daily discourse reveal the lie in such an assertion? Oh, you are yet of an earthly, sensual spirit! The spirit of this world is yet bearing rule in you. Your very soul is but a lump of earth and flesh. Oh, for another spirit, a new soul, a more divine and celestial frame! Oh, seek and wait for this better spirit, and then you may quickly see another life! Once let the world be thrust out from the heart, and then you may quickly see more of heaven breaking forth in the life.

Oh, you worldlings, start up out of your security and slumber! Will you receive the Word of the Lord and allow yourselves to be convinced? Will you believe yourselves to be unbelievers? Open your eyes. View the whole course of your lives, and let your conscience speak freely.

Never talk of Christianity till you cease to be worldlings. And never consider that you are less worldlings until you understand better what is the great salvation wrought out by the Lord Jesus Christ for poor sinners, that which He offers freely and graciously to sinners.

If these two things might affect your hearts (that you are of the world and that they who are of the world have no part with Christ), then there would be hope that you would accept these counsels which we now give you in Christian affection.

According to the truth or falsehood of your faith, so shall you be either conquerors of or captives to the world. Every unbeliever is a captive of the world; every believer is a conqueror of the world.

Faith makes more full and experimental discoveries of the glory of that inheritance which the soul has pitched upon. There is no way possible to divide the heart from this world till it shall choose a better. Whatever it finds and apprehends to be good, that it grasps and will hold till a higher good come in sight.

The world is considered by the worldling to be his treasure. It is the best he knows, and he must be bought out of it before he will let it go. He must be bought out of his house, his riches, his comforts, and his pleasures by something that is apprehended to be a valuable price before he will choose to quit what he has. It is vain to persuade him to voluntary poverty, unless he has in view a higher good. All the arguments from the insufficiency and instability, the vanity and vexation of earthly things will be easily answered by the worldling. He will say, "But where shall I have better? It is better to have half a loaf than no bread; a short meal is better than starving." The heart will not let go of this world but upon the discovery of a better.

According to the degree of manifestation of those better things above, so will there be more or less an abatement of our affection to things below. Even as a little light from heaven will make the world look dim, and the sun rising higher will make all our stars creep into darkness; so, at the first entrance of the illuminating, mighty influence of the Holy Spirit into the soul, the world loses its place and is thrust lower and lower as the love of God rises higher, till, at length, it is brought quite under foot.

It is impossible that God and the world should be supremely loved together. That both should be our aim and chief good is a contradiction. It is irrational for any to conclude that they have any proper respect for God if they are strongly attached to the world. Many professors of religion may be convinced that their religion is vain by this—that, to whatever height it seems to be raised, it is overtopped by their earthly-mindedness. "If any man love the world, the love of the Father is not in him," 1 John 2:15.

Victory consists in living by faith.

Faith, in its entrance into the soul, brings this tiding—that God is better than the world—and, as it grows higher, so accordingly is its testimony to this truth more clear and full. As the Apostle said concerning the righteousness of God, Romans 1:17, so is it true of His goodness, kindness, mercy, and all-sufficiency. The goodness and kindness of God is revealed from faith to faith. That is, as faith grows, so accordingly is God and all the excellencies of His glorious name more known. Every cubit added to the stature of our faith is a new beam of light sprung forth from the face of God, and God known is heaven known, our blessedness and our inheritance known. God is our inheritance.

Faith is the good spy (see Numbers 13) which is sent forth to view the promised land. The devil's spy is sense. Now sense must go and inquire concerning the inheritance of the saints. But it, being short-sighted and not able to travel far, takes up all its tidings on hearsay; and, finding no good report among all its acquaintances (sensual men will never speak well of the things of God), it hereupon returns with this evil report—that it is a dark, dry, and barren land; that there is nothing of what is good and delightful to be found in it; and everlasting joy and rest are represented by it to be mere fancies and conceits. Then, sense determines that it is better to abide here in this world, for here are houses, lands, and pleasures. It knows that there are, and sees that there are, these things, but what there is in the other world is altogether dark and uncertain to it.

Has sense never dealt thus by you? What apprehensions have you of the glory to come? Has not your blind sense disparaged and disgraced the things of the Kingdom of God to you? You take everything to be as sense judges it, and what is the judgment of sense of these glorious things? It speaks highly of things temporal. This world is good, a land flowing with milk and honey, but what does it say concerning things eternal? Are none of you the men and women whose sensual hearts have told you (and you have believed them) that it is uncertain whether there is a heaven or not? Or, if you are persuaded that there is, yet the happiness of it is so much unknown that, if you could, it would be more to your contentment to live your eternity among your sheep and oxen, amidst your shops or palaces, or in these gardens and orchards, in the possession of your earthly delights and pleasures, than ever to be carried hence to that unknown world.

Your opinions of these higher things, we may guess at by the care you take about them. What care is taken by you about the things of God? What is there done by you about these matters? Have you taken up any design for heaven and are you taking any effectual course for eternal blessedness? Are you as hearty and serious in seeking God as you have been in seeking the world? While your hearts are so hot, so zealous, and so busy in pursuing things temporal, is it not a matter of indifference to you whether you do anything, or how you do it in seeking the Kingdom of God? Do you pray, labor, and watch for your souls with as good a will as ever you worked for your living? Do you hunger and thirst after the knowledge and grace of God, after Christ, after the pardon of your sins as ever you do after your appointed food?

Do you, each one of you, inquire, "How is it with me? What evidence do I have for heaven? Have I any right to the tree of life? Is there no fear I may fall short of the rest and be shut out of the Kingdom of God? How may I know whether I am a disciple of Christ or not?" Perhaps your sense has so much disparaged things to come that they are to you as if they were hardly worth inquiring after.

But, now, faith is the good spy that makes good report of the promised land. It makes more diligent search after the riches of it, finds out its hidden treasures, and then speaks as it finds. Faith has a glass wherein it can behold and whereby it reveals to the soul the glory of God. The gospel is its glass, 2 Corinthians 3:18. The great and precious promises are the deeds and conveyances by which this inheritance is made over. Now, as among men in their legal deeds there is mention made of all the particulars made over by them—the houses, the lands, the forests, the rivers, the royalties, and all the immunities belonging thereto—so these promises are written assurances of valuable possessions; and faith is frequently looking into them and reading over the writings and, thence, understands what a glorious purchase it has made.

Nay, more, faith brings down some of the fruits of this good land. Faith comes in laden with goodly clusters for Canaan.

God, now and then, lets fall to a true Christian who walks with Him some handfuls of the harvest, some drops of that vintage which is ripening for him above. What are those beams of divine light, that sense of divine love, those intimations of divine acceptance, those communications of the divine image in the increases of holiness and righteousness, and that joy of faith and peace in believing? What are these but specimens of heaven, the first fruits of glory?

By faith, the kingdom of heaven is within us. There is God within us, Christ within us, and glory within us. Those believers who live in the power of faith and holiness need not travel far in search for heaven; it is but looking inward, and there they may find it. Say not, "O blessed man, who shall ascend in search for heaven?" It is in your heart. Sinners need not go down to the deep to search for hell, there is a hell within them—the filth and savor of hell in their vile affections, the smoke and flames of hell in their reeking and burning lusts, the darkness of hell in their debased and blinded minds, and, sometimes, the torments of hell in the anguish of their guilty and self-avenging consciences. As sinners may find a hell, so believers may find a heaven in the heart; a heaven of light, a heaven of love, joy, and praise. Thus it is with some, and thus it might be with all, were they strong in faith.

Alas! What we lose living by sense when we might live by faith! How have our sensual hearts, by consuming and spinning out our days in sloth and idleness, halting at the labor of duty, whining under difficulties, shrinking from sufferings, indulging in our ease, our pleasures, and our liberties—how our sensual hearts have robbed us of the life of God, the happiness of angels, and the joys of heaven and left us little more of Christianity than its wounds and bruises, its mournings and complainings, its sighs and sorrows! O foolish hearts that consult so unwisely for yourselves; that choose rather to live in bushes, among these briars and thorns, than among the beds of spices; that will rather languish in a wilderness than get you up to the garden of the Lord!

The life of faith is a heavenly life; though faith shall never come into heaven itself, yet it is by faith that saints attain to heaven. Faith came down from heaven, it is the gift of God; and, though it must not return there (for it is love and not faith that shall swell before the throne of God), yet there it raises those hearts in which it lives.

Dear friends, be serious. Feel your own pulses, view your own ways, search your own hearts, and see where your daily thoughts are. May you not find them, hundreds of times, walking to and fro through the earth, for the one time that they cast a look towards heaven?

What is the work which you follow every day? Instead of being vessels of honor, waiting before the throne of God, standing in His courts, bearing His name, beholding His face, setting forth His praises, have you not been hewers of wood, drawers of water, servers of tables, purveyors for the flesh, caterers for the appetite, laying in provision for your own lusts? Are not these your heart-work? When anything is to be done for God, the body must do it. The body will go to the temple or the closet, the tongue will pray, the ear will hear, the eye will read, but the soul must wander away. But when the flesh is to be served, that is the heartwork, that is the work which engages the man.

Victory consists in being crucified with Christ.

Consider, then, is this faith? Is this the victory over the world? Is this to be mortified? Is this to be crucified with Christ or to have your conversation in heaven? Can you think yourselves to be believers when you are so earthly?

What do you think of those Jews, of whom the Lord speaks, "They come unto thee as the people cometh, and they sit before thee as My people, and they hear thy words, but they will not do them: for with their mouth they shew much love, but their heart goeth after their covetousness," Ezekiel 33:31. These are not the people of God, whose religion is merely to hear and to pray, who have a mouth speaking love to God but a heart full of covetousness.

Let us consider those words of Scripture wherein the Apostle Paul spoke with tears in his eyes of professors of an earthly sort: "Many walk, of whom I have told you often, and now tell you even weeping, that they are the enemies of the cross of Christ: whose end is destruction, whose god is their belly, and whose glory is in their shame, who mind earthly things," Philippians 3:18-19.

In the former part of the chapter, you may observe how the Apostle gives an account of himself and his own Christianity in these particulars:

1. He set such a high value on Christ and felt such an interest in His righteousness that, in comparison thereof, he counted all things else but loss for the excellency of the knowledge of Christ Jesus, his Lord, for whom he had suffered the loss of all things.

2. He united interest in Christ with conformity to

Christ, and his soul was trying to attain both in the same breath. He said, "That I may win Christ, and be found in Him . . . that I may know Him, and the power of His resurrection, and the fellowship of His sufferings, being made conformable unto His death," Philippians 3:8-10. He would not only rejoice in Christ, he would not only live in Christ but be dead with Christ and then be raised with Christ above these earthly things. He would have his interest in the death and resurrection of Christ witnessed by fellowship with Him in both, by the power of His death and resurrection made manifest in him. He would that both the death of Jesus and the life of Jesus should be made manifest in him.

3. He set his face and bent his whole course towards the obtaining of an interest in Christ. He said, "I press toward the mark for the prize of the high calling of God in Christ Jesus," Philippians 3:14, and this not in his prayers only but in his whole practice. Again, he said, "This one thing I do, forgetting those things which are behind, and reaching forth unto those things which are before," Philippians 3:13. This one thing was all. Whatever he was doing, this he was doing. He had nothing else to do, nothing else to seek, but conformity to Christ. He turned his back upon all things else, forgetting those things which are behind— that is, not only his former attainments but also all worldly and earthly things.

4. He said, "Yea doubtless, and I count all things but loss," Philippians 3:8. He left all behind. First, he set his feet upon them and trod them down, and then he turned back upon them and left them all behind. Henceforth, his whole conversation was heavenward.

He said, "Our conversation is in heaven," Philippians 3:20. Lo! This is the man who was bold to say, "But God forbid that I should glory, save in the cross of our Lord Jesus Christ, by whom the world is crucified unto me, and I unto the world," Galatians 6:14.

5. He pointed at some among the Philippians who professed to follow Christ but walked not after Christ. Here are the men and here is their censure; here is their mark and their brand, their mark and description: "The enemies of the cross of Christ . . . who mind earthly things." Here is their doom: "Whose end is destruction."

Professors, are your hearts and ways as the hearts of these? So shall your judgment be. You may say as the Apostle, "We are the circumcision. We are Christ's, who worship God in the Spirit and rejoice in Christ Jesus, and have no confidence in the flesh," Philippians 3:3. But, yet, have you not fellowship with the flesh? Do you not walk after the flesh, even while you pretend to rejoice in Christ Jesus and to worship God in the Spirit?

And how many such marked and branded disciples may we find among us whom, while their lusts have marked them as earthly-minded, the Word of God brands as enemies and vessels of destruction. While the devil and the world have branded the whole generation of the saints as a proud, deceitful, hypocritical, and self-seeking generation, Christ has set this brand on worldly persons—earthly, sensual, devilish.

Oh, if we could speak of these with the heart of the Apostle, we should speak with his tears also! We should, weeping, speak that they are the enemies of the cross of Christ, that they are the shame and the reproach of the profession of the gospel, and through them the gospel is wounded!

Alas! How many enemies has the cross of Christ made Him? Oh, how few friends have the calls which Christ has made to come out from an evil world left Him? Are those the friends of Christ who are the enemies of His cross? Are those the friends of Christ who are the familiars of the world? Will professing, praying, and hearing baptize such into the name of disciples? If lying and promise-breaking, if serving and satiating of appetites, if pride, fullness of bread, and abundance of covetous labor were the marks of disciples, we might find them walking on every side—whole towns and whole countries of them. If these were to be reckoned as disciples, how great a herd would the little flock become? If those swine that are rooting in the earth or wallowing in the mire must all go for lambs, if these sensualists and worldly-minded persons must all be thrown into the number, if the wise of the world, the politicians and speculators, must all pass under the same name, to what a bulk would the fold swell! But, since all these must be set aside as none of the sheep, what a small flock will then be left!

Be not deceived; God is not mocked. As you sow, so shall you also reap. Your sowing to the flesh, even while you boast of the Spirit, is conviction enough whose you are and what your end will be, whose end is destruction.

But one who is of the world may say, "I mean not to cast away my confidence; far be it from me that I should think that I have professed in vain, that I have heard, prayed, and believed all this while in vain. I know in whom I have believed. I feel that I love God.

Whatever corruptions I have, I am persuaded that nothing shall separate me from the love of God, which is in Christ Jesus my Lord, and I will not cast away my confidence."

The meaning of all these good words may be no more than this, that he will hold his opinion against the strongest evidence of Scripture and reason. For what is that which he calls the witness and the seal of the Spirit but an opinion of his own, a strong persuasion of his heart, that he is a child of God. Because it is attested by some desires after heaven, he takes it to be the voice of the Holy Spirit, though it is never so contradictory to the Word of God. So he will hold his confidence, notwithstanding what the Word of God says to the contrary.

Victory consists in being sealed by the Spirit.

The Holy Spirit seals the disciples of Christ by setting His mark upon them. It is written, "He that keepeth His commandments dwelleth in Him, and He in him, and hereby we know that He abideth in us, by the Spirit which He hath given us," 1 John 3:24. The Spirit of God forms saints into His own likeness, and this image of the Spirit is the mark of God upon them.

As men's sheep, so the sheep of Christ may be known by their Master's mark upon them. Whose mark is that of an earthly mind? Is it not the mark of the god of this world? Holiness and spirituality is the mark of Christ; earthliness and sin is the mark of the devil. To whom does your soul belong? The Spirit, you may say, witnesses that you belong to God. Aye, but whose mark is it that is upon you? This covetousness and greediness

after the world, this lying and defrauding, this unrighteousness and unmercifulness to which the world can
ordinarily tempt you, these are the devil's marks.

It is true, Christ takes each one of His sheep out of
the devil's flock; but whatever sheep He brings home,
He blots out the old and stamps His own mark upon it.
Though there are some stains of the old still remaining
(which, until flesh is put off, will remain), yet the new
mark which Christ has set on now decidedly prevails.

Say not that you are sealed by the Holy Spirit, whatever your comforts or confidences have been, unless
you see His mark upon you. Say not that you are
marked by the Spirit while the devil's mark, an earthly
mind, is most visible and conspicuous upon you.

The Holy Spirit also seals the disciples of Christ by
being the light of the Lord within them, whereby they
are able to discern the Lord's mark upon them. The
Apostle Paul thus wrote to a Christian church, "Now we
have received, not the spirit of the world, but the Spirit
which is of God; that we might know the things that
are freely given to us of God," 1 Corinthians 2:12.

How the devil deludes souls.

The devil so bewilders and deludes souls that they
often know not what to make of themselves but conclude themselves to be quite another thing than they
are. This he does in the following ways:

By counterfeiting Christ's mark and setting it upon
his own servants.

By making his own mark to appear to be the true
one.

By endeavoring to blot and deface Christ's mark, so

that it cannot easily be seen or known to be his.

First, the devil deludes by counterfeiting Christ's mark and setting it upon his own servants. The Lord Jesus Christ marks His sheep especially in the heart, which is the throne of the Spirit. The heart is the seat of grace. The devil can, in some degree, counterfeit this. He can make common grace look like saving grace; he can paint the face of a saint upon the heart of a sinner.

He can counterfeit the outward marks of Christ. Christ has His outward marks. His earmark is, "My sheep hear My voice," John 10:27; His mark in the forehead, the owning or confessing of Christ before men: "Whosoever shall confess Me before men, him shall the Son of Man also confess before the angels of God," Luke 12:8; His mark in the mouth, that God makes His people of a pure language, Zephaniah 3:9. The devil can counterfeit this. He can bring his flock to hear the preaching of the gospel; he can bring them to make a sort of confession of Christ; he can teach them to pray and to be expert in the language of disciples; and, when he has done this, then he suggests to them that they belong to Christ for, behold, they pray and acknowledge Christ. Yet, notwithstanding, whatever may be upon the ear, the tongue, or the forehead, the image of the devil is still upon the heart.

Second, the devil deludes by making his own mark to appear to be the true one. Do you think that you have Christ's mark upon you? Aye, but whose mark is that of an earthly mind, which appears stamped upon you? Oh, but the devil can delude here too! He has a cloak for covetousness. He will suggest to you that this earthly-mindedness is but prudence and good hus-

bandry; nay, that very gain is holiness; and that all this
caring and drudging for the world is but in obedience
to the command of God to provide for yourselves or
families. In this, the devil is so successful that it is one
of the hardest tasks to convince poor worldlings of the
delusion, though all who know them clearly perceive
that they are but earthly-minded and engaged in his
service.

Third, the devil deludes by endeavoring to blot and
deface Christ's mark so that it cannot easily be seen or
known to be His. As he makes a mere pretense look
like sincerity, so he makes sincerity look like hypocrisy.
As many worldlings bless themselves in the opinion of
their uprightness, so some mortified, broken, upright
hearts condemn themselves as unfaithful. Though
Christ is in them and has set His seal upon their hearts,
yet the devil raises up so many dark mists of melan-
choly thoughts and fears that they cannot well perceive
what there is of Christ in them. And, thereupon, they
judge very sadly of their case. So one of such may,
mourning, say, "I fear that I am mistaken, and that I
am none of Christ's, for what is there of the grace of
Christ in me?"

But, as the Holy Ghost works grace in the heart, so
He gives light to the eyes. He opens the Scriptures and
shows to the soul the mark of Christ. He enlightens the
mind and shows the very same mark, which is written
in the Word, stamped upon the soul; and, thereby, he
establishes it in power. But, if there is no such mark
found there, the peace that is talked of is not of the
Spirit of God but of the devil.

Worldly professors! Do you not see the Scripture
death-mark upon you? Or, if you do not, do not they

who know you perceive it? Does not this earthly mind
appear upon your foreheads, upon your tongues, upon
the palms of your hands, and upon the prints of your
feet? May not your love of the world be read in your
looks, in your words, and in the lines of your lives; and
will you yet say that it is the Spirit of the Lord that
speaks peace to you? Does not this foul, hateful, awful
mark belong to you? Will you, now, still be deceived in
persuading yourselves that you have received the Spirit
of adoption? It is folly and worse than folly. It is
wickedness to boast that you belong to Christ, that you
have the Spirit of Christ, that you are risen with Christ,
while your hearts have gotten no farther up out of
their graves.

Recollect that the hand and seal of God agree. His
Word does not write, "I do not know you," while His
Spirit seals that man a child of God. See and compare
the testimony of God with that which is in your hearts.
If the voice within you does not accord with the Word
of God, it is not the witness of the Holy Ghost, but the
witness of the devil.

Of those who make a fair profession of devoting
themselves to Christ as their Lord, confessing Him,
and giving up all for Him, how few are there whose affections do not run down to earth? Though they have
professed to count this earth but dross, yet, at the same
time, they are too greedily gathering it up. They have
far more of earth in their hearts than they are aware
of. They are not willing to lose what they have actually
professed to account "but loss."

Even among too many of you who consider that
you are, indeed, the disciples of Christ, there appears
too little conformity to the life of Christ. While your

eyes are towards heaven, you creep too much upon the earth. There is in you such a wavering between earth and heaven that it is hard to discern which has the upper hand. Your time, care, and labor run out so much on worldly things that it might appear that your hearts were more engaged with earth than heaven.

Do you then blush at your unworthiness? Are you not ashamed that such love and such mercy should not more wean your too wayward hearts from the paths of vanity, that you should make so light of heavenly treasure, and that you should so disgrace your Father's table by your appetite after the husks of the world? Has your profession that God is your happiness, your treasure, your all, come to no more than this? Has your covenanting with God for renouncing the world, mortifying your flesh, and denying yourselves brought forth no better fruits than these? Oh, how great is the pride and deadness of your hearts, that can carry the consciousness of such treachery before the throne of God without shame and consternation! How can you appear before the Lord without hanging down your heads?

Dear friends, no longer dishonor God nor delude yourselves. Let not the world any longer say to your reproach, "These men are even as we are." Let them see that your ways are not as their ways, that your joys are not as their joys; and then they may know that your hope is not as their hope, your Rock is not as their rock.

Search within your hearts for the proof of your heavenly extraction. Have no patience with yourselves while you are such degenerate plants. Rest not satisfied that you are the children of God, when you are so unlike Him. How can you, without weeping, behold the glory of these latter days, and fall so far short of those who were in the ages before you? Consider the spirituality, the mortification, and self-denial of the primitive Christians.

Alas! How many may now lament to themselves, "Oh, how earthly have we become! Our gold is mixed with dross, our beauty with ashes; our spirit partakes too much of flesh. How hard we are driving after bags of riches! We seek too anxiously for the things of this world. When riches increase, there are but few to be found who do not set their hearts upon them. Who is there who labors to be as holy as to be rich, to thrive in holiness as in riches? Though the Lord has taken off our chariot wheels, still we drive on. Though He has burnt up our houses, yet our hearts are still among the rubbish. Though He has mingled wormwood with our milk and gall with our honey, yet we say it is sweet and will not be weaned from what we so love. Though God has testified against our pride and our covetousness, and made such stains upon our beauty and such wasting in our bags of wealth, though God is angry with us, angry for the iniquity of our covetousness, yet who among us has given up the eager pursuit of the world? Oh, what is likely to become of us?"

But if we should hear complaints of this kind and let fall a tear for the guilty, may they not turn upon us and say, "Weep not for us but for yourselves; for your own covetousness, for your own worldly-mindedness." And what should we say for ourselves if they did so? Might we not say, "Oh, in strict truth, we are of the company. We, even we, also are guilty. This idol has a tabernacle in our hearts also, though we have too little considered it."

But must our complaints suffice us? Is it enough to make all well that we confess matters to be so bad? Must this be all our heavenliness, to bewail our earthliness? Will God take our acknowledgments for amendments? Is this our redemption, to bewail our captivity? But when shall it be better? When shall it be said to these prisoners, "Go forth"? When for the other world, for God alone, for nothing but Christ and His everlasting kingdom? Arise, O captives, put off your prison garments. Get up out of your houses of bondage. Unfetter your spirits. Get your feet out of the snare and away for heaven. Leave this earth to its heirs. Let the men of this world take it as their portion and be the only servants of it, but you go and serve the Lord. While worldlings will not be the servants of Christ, let the saints show that they are not the servants of the world.

Dear friends, conclude that you have no more of Christianity than you have of spirituality; that every admitted spot of earthliness will, unavoidably, be a blot upon your evidences for heaven.

Whatever arguments worldly men may have in their favor, yet how many objections are there also? How many "buts" are there against them? Such a one is considered to be a judicious and understanding Christian, *but* he is greedy for the world; such a one is of a courteous behavior, *but* he is unkind to the poor; such a one is much in prayer, *but* there is no confidence to be placed in his word; such a one is of a free and liberal spirit, *but* he is proud.

Dear friends, receive the word of conviction and submit to it. The sum whereof is that, where there is so much of the spirit of this world, there is but little, if any, faith.

Now, will you choose to stay at the brick-kilns of Egypt or will you go over to Canaan? What are your resolutions? Will you enjoy Christian liberty or not? Have you not understood enough of the world's tyranny, and have you not sinned and suffered enough already by it? What say you? Are you for liberty or bondage? For captivity or victory?

Study to have the right judgment of both worlds, and do not give up this study till you are thoroughly convinced of the unspeakable superiority of things to come above things present.

Take advantage of all those means by which your faith may gather strength, and in which its strength may be put forth and exercised.

Carry the sense of your sore bondage into the presence of God. Let the misery and danger it has subjected you to be written upon your hearts and go and spread the writing before the Lord. Make your humble confession of your too fond attachment to the world before the Almighty God. Make it your constant prayer that He will, by His grace, strengthen you to resist the world.

Speak to the Lord, do not let your souls keep silent. Let your oppressed hearts lift up their voices to Him. Ask God to create in you a clean heart and to renew a right spirit within you. Ask Him for a new heart that may not find pleasure, nay, nor so much as ease, in such things as the world has to offer.

If you have gotten a little ground, take the same way to maintain what you have gotten. If the world rallies against you, and your affections begin to stoop to

it, then seek strength in prayer. If your hearts begin
again to wander after it, and your corruptions and
temptations begin to get ahead again and prevail, meet
them with a prayer at every turn. "May the Lord rebuke
you, false heart. May the Lord rebuke you, deceitful
world. May the Lord uphold you, oppressed soul."

Dear friends, your victory over the world can neither be gotten nor maintained but by a power derived
from the Holy Ghost. In vain do you engage in the
conflict unless He engages with you. Prayer will set
faith to work, faith will insure the promise, the promise
will engage Christ with you, and Christ will engage the
Father to your help. As heaven is superior to earth, so
the world shall fall before a faithful, praying soul.

Take now this counsel—as you find the world to be
your great enemy, bend the force of prayer in your
contest against it. And each of you, whenever you have
made your prayer, judge the acceptance of it by the
success it has against the world.

When, at any time, you have found your soul most
melted and enlarged in prayer and greatly refreshed by
sensible incomes from above, at such a time presently
demand, "But how stands it now with the interest of
the world in me? How stands my heart now affected to
worldly things? Am I weaned from the world? Is my
clog fallen off? What have my earthly-mindedness, my
covetousness, and my other evil affections lost in this
prayer? Can I now go away and be contented and patient in any condition? Am I less care-filled and less
concerned which way the world goes with me; or can I
go down presently to my business and after my pursuits
and be as hungry after and as much swallowed up of
my earthly cares and delights as if I had never tasted

anything of the favor and goodness of God? If so, I must not be content with this. I must go to prayer again and again. While I live, I will not give over. I will wrestle, I will wait, I will inquire after every prayer, 'Is it yet better with me? Am I yet more mortified, yet more spiritual, yet more humble and contented?' I will never satisfy myself with any praying while the world has power over me."

Keeping the Sabbath strengthens the warrior.

Keep holy the Sabbath-day. There is, in the ordinances of this day, a means of strengthening and refreshment for the soul. Seek, by the grace of God, to renew your strength for warfare against the world.

The Sabbath should be a day of separation for God. This day is a hallowed day, sanctified by God, and to be sanctified by His saints. God, in sanctifying it, set it apart for a holy use; our sanctifying it is our setting ourselves apart, thereon, for His holy service. This day is a privileged day, and nothing that is common should encroach upon it.

You are, then, in the fairest way for victory over the world when you are farthest from it. While it is in your eye or in your hand, it is not easy to keep it out of your hearts; but accordingly, as you commune with the Most High God, the world will lose its hold and power over you.

But the reason why men ordinarily make no more advantage of Sabbath is because, however they pretend to draw nigh unto God, they do not withdraw from the world. They too often carry all they have with them when they come up to the house of the Lord. The low-

ing of the oxen, the bleating of the sheep, and the
sound of the millstones is still so in their ears; the but-
ter and the honey, the wine and the oil, the silver and
the gold are still so continually in their view that they
cannot hearken and attend to what the Lord God
speaks in His Word and ordinances.

Dear friends, who is there with you in the Sabbath-
hour? When you are in the place of worship, who is
there with you? Search, look into every corner of your
hearts. Is there someone within who should not be
there? Is there no messenger of Satan? Has the world
no partisans at work within you? Oh, behold, while the
Lord is calling you to take your thoughts off the world
and to hold communion with Him, what a mixed multitude are there within—cares, thoughts, desires, and
projects for this world—and what a stir they all make so
that God may not be regarded!

It is no wonder that the seed dies and becomes unfruitful which falls into a brake of thorns or among
such birds as stand watching to catch it all away. What
hope is there that the counsel of the Lord will be accepted by a mind taken up and filled with the cares of
this life?

You can never ascend with your burden upon your
backs. Unload, unload. Lay aside every weight, and
then go up and prosper!

On this day, empty your hands. Come in from your
fields; come out from your shops; lay down your work;
leave the business of this earth below; come up to meet
your God.

Dear friends, where is your Sabbath separation? Is
there not a fault among you upon this account? Let
each inquire, "How it is with me? Am I not faulty?

What are my Sabbath thoughts, my Sabbath dis-
courses? What are my morning, evening, and midday
thoughts? What is my table-talk and my fireside-talk on
this holy day? If business, bargains, or journeys are not
admitted, are not visits, compliments, vain stories, or
impertinent news suffered to fill up the time?"

Clear your Sabbaths of such worldly encroachments
or your hearts will never be cleared. Drive all the world
into banishment and be wholly in the Spirit on the
Lord's day. Be abstracted from earthly things and
earthly thoughts. Do not bring them with you to the
house or to the day of the Lord. Let your own houses
and your own tables be as the house and table of the
Lord. Make it your business and delight from morning
to evening to wait upon God.

Say to all your goods, "Lie by here while I go and
pray before the Lord." Let the night before each
Sabbath be as the grave between the two worlds. There
let your dust be buried and your spirit fly unburdened
to your God. Let that night, which is the partition between common days and the Lord's day, be your soul's
taking its leave of all you have; not only of matters
which are sinful, but of matters also which are lawful
and honest, that concern this earth. Charge them not
to thrust in before the Lord. And if, from Sabbath to
Sabbath, your feet stand thus on the mountain of the
Lord, you may find them all the week long overtopping
the mountains of the earth.

The Sabbath is a day for special communion with
God. The meeting of God with His people on that day
is like that meeting which was promised to Moses before the mercy seat. God said to him, "There will I
meet with thee, and I will commune with thee from

above the mercy seat, from between the two cherubims which are upon the ark of the testimony, of all things which I will give thee in commandment unto the children of Israel," Exodus 25:22.

Dear friends, have you ever experienced Sabbath-communion? Have there been friendly and familiar intercourses between God and your souls? Oh, how contemptible does the world and all its riches and pleasures appear, in the eyes of those who hold communion with God on this blessed day!

But our Sabbaths are too often dark and cloudy days to us. What dry feasts, too often, are our Sabbath feasts. They are rather fasts than feasts. Real communion with God is too strange a thing to us, even on the day of God. Heaven is opened, but our eyes are too often shut. God comes down to meet us and to bless us, but our hearts are too often away from Him. Our Sabbaths are but, too often, the shadows of Sabbaths.

In the morning of the Sabbath consider, "This is the day which the Lord hath made; we will rejoice and be glad in it," Psalm 118:24. Climb up quickly and let every duty be a step by which, through faith, you may ascend to God. Let divine contemplation, prayers, and praises be your whole work. Let the blessing of divine communion be the whole expectation of that day; and, when you find your hearts refreshed with the presence and filled with the communion of your God, and He sends you away laden with the tokens of His love, the impress of His grace, and the relish of His goodness fresh upon your hearts, then you may learn to despise the matters of sense, of business, and of pleasure with which the world has sought to entertain you. Then, regarding pomps and pleasures, houses and lands, you will say, "We have enough. We have held communion with our God, in whose presence is fullness of joy and at whose right hand there are pleasures forevermore."

He who is not prepared to meet his Lord and Master is not prepared to meet his adversary, the devil, in spiritual warfare.

It is no wonder that the world overcomes you who go for days, perhaps for years, without heavenly food for your souls. When your souls are famished into weakness, then you may become an easy prey to your enemies. They are the hunger-starved sheep that are a prey to wild birds and animals. If Satan can but keep you low, if he can keep you idle when you should be gathering heavenly manna, he may then lead you after his lure at pleasure. It is not a little strength that will suffice you against his great temptations, and it is not a little bread by which you are likely to gather any great strength. You have need to eat well if you will be strong, and you have need to be strong or you will never be able to contend manfully against the devil.

Remember your Creator and rest from your works, as God did from His. Remember your Redeemer and rise from your dust, as Christ rose from the dead. Let this day of His resurrection be the day of your resurrection. Let Sabbaths be Sabbaths indeed, holy to the Lord and entirely His. Let this day be, to your souls, entirely the Lord's day.

Observing the Lord's Supper
strengthens the warrior.

There is also, in the ordinance of the Lord's supper, one great means for the strengthening and re-
freshing of the soul for warfare against the world.

With regard to this ordinance, self-examination is a
marked duty. It is written, "But let a man examine himself, and so let him eat of that bread, and drink of that
cup," 1 Corinthians 11:28. The world works its work of
death in the soul with much secrecy. It has its covert
places in which it lurks unseen. Yet this enemy lies not
so close but that it may be discovered by a close and
faithful search and trial. Now, this examination-trial
should be close and thorough; no corner within your
hearts should be left unexamined. The dreadful consequence of coming so solemnly before the Lord with
a traitor in your bosoms should cry in your ears, "Make
diligent search."

The evidence that this one thing, an earthly mind,
carries in it treachery and hypocrisy towards God is so
notorious that he can have but little understanding in
the religion of Christ who would not, from this alone,
conclude himself an unworthy guest at the table of the
Lord, were all things else ever so specious and fair.

Get the sense of these awful truths upon your
hearts, that he who eats and drinks unworthily is guilty
of the body and blood of Christ, and that he that eats
and drinks unworthily eats and drinks condemnation
to himself; that he who is an idolater eats and drinks
unworthily, and that he who is covetous is an idolater.
Then see if you dare to come to the Lord's table with-

out a deep search into your hearts.

Oh, you professors! What care do you commonly take of this duty? Do you examine yourselves? Do you make diligent search after sin? Oh, then, let one and another make such an inquiry as this: "Have I faith in Christ? Have I a thankful remembrance of His death? Have I charity? Do I bear any malice? Am I unjust? Am I an oppressor or an extortioner? Have I done wrong to any man? Do I not love the world more than God; is not my heart too much upon it? Am I not too busy for the world? Is not my time spent too much upon it? Are not duties neglected for it? Is not my soul, or the souls of my family, neglected for its sake? Am I not so bent upon growing rich in the world that I mind not how poverty has grown upon my soul? Do I honor the Lord with my substance? Am I merciful? Am I bountiful to others? Do I seek no more than God would have me otherwise to seek? Do I strive to serve God with all that I am and all that I have? Do I know how to abound? Can I endure want, if the Lord will have it so? Is God a sufficient portion for me? How can I bear crosses and disappointments in the world?"

Now, there is a time to reply to these heart-searching inquiries. Lose not the season; beware of solemn triflings; beware of palliating your sins; be zealous to know the worst of your case; be faithful to your consciences. What say you, guilty or not guilty?

Repentance, if it is sincere, will be universal. It will extend to every known sin. He who does not repent of everything that is evil truly repents of nothing.

Repentance has respect not only to the time to come, but also to the time past. What has been done cannot, properly speaking, be undone; but, in one sense, it may. Heartily wishing it to be undone is, in God's acceptance through Christ, an undoing of it; and the wishing from the heart all evil that has been done to be undone is essential to true repentance. But can anyone be said to have repented that he has been a worldling who would not, for anything, wish that he had not been so? Has he repented who, if he were to begin again, would take the same course?

Now, however difficult it may be for him whose heart has hitherto gone after his covetousness to depart from it, yet, in this, there is much more difficulty to heartily wish that he had never been guilty of any covetous practices in the first place. Such an undoing of his sin might be his undoing in the matter of his estate or property.

It may be that his covetousness has brought him his whole living and obtained for him all the property he has in the world. If he had not been an oppressor, or a fraudulent dealer, or a devoted servant of the world, possibly he would have been but a poor man to this day and never acquired wealth. His house, his money, and his lands are all the product of his covetousness. To wish that he had been true, honest, and conscientious in the transactions of his life may be the same as to wish himself in perpetual poverty.

No doubt the drunkard may readily wish, "Oh that I had ever been sober!" The prodigal may wish, "Oh, that I had never thus foolishly wasted my estate!" But will the covetous man easily wish, "Oh, that I had never thus gotten an estate?" Yet all this is essential to repentance.

It is not as hard a trial for a rich man, who now has enough, to be required to covet no more, to be unjust no longer, and never again to neglect God or his soul for his worldly interest; for, even if he is ever so strict this way for the future, his flesh is not likely to suffer so much by it, as he has enough already to feed it. But to wish his money out of his purse, to wish himself back to that low state from which his fraud or covetousness raised him; yea, to wish this so as to be ready to refund and to make restitution of all his dishonest gains—this is a hard trial, but must be endured by one who seeks to come to Christ. Such a one should beware how he goes on heaping up riches. The Sacrament of the Lord's Supper is called the new testament: "This cup is the new testament in My blood," Luke 22:20.

The New Testament is heaven opened; it is life and immortality brought to light by the gospel. It is our Lord's last will, wherein we may read what rich and glorious legacies He has bequeathed to His saints.

This Sacrament is thus a lively representation of the great blessings of the covenant; it presents Christ crucified before our eyes. It is a commemoration of Christ crucified. Sometimes, you know, dying friends bequeath unto their dear survivors some token of their love, a ring or a seal; some token to preserve their memory. So our dying Lord bequeathed this signet, this evidence of Himself crucified, to His living saints with this charge: "This do in remembrance of Me," Luke 22:19.

This Sacrament is the showing forth of Christ's death till He comes, 1 Corinthians 11:26. In His cross may be seen the crown. You may judge the purchase by the price that was paid for it. The pardons, the peace, the hopes, the robes, the mansions, the inheritance incorruptible and undefiled to which saints are re-

deemed, they have a survey of them all in this price
that was paid for them. The love of Christ, His kindnesses and compassions, are all presented to them. His
tears, His stripes, His grief, His groans, and His blood
all say, "Behold, how He loved us! Behold, what He has
laid up for those who love Him!"

Dear friends, shall not this price buy off your souls
from earth, which is sufficient to buy them off from
hell? You have been at the table of the Lord; but,
surely, you do not perceive or meet Jesus there, if your
souls yet dwell in the dust.

What! Have you no eyes to see the glory of Christ?
What! See it and not desire it? What! Still feeding on
earth? Look till you see and see till you love Him; then
ascend and be satisfied. Our blessed Lord said, "And I,
if I be lifted up from the earth, will draw all men unto
Me," John 12:32. Now, then, is the Son of Man presented before you. What are your hearts, if they do not
begin to ascend?

Our blessed Lord, in giving to His people the
Sacramental elements, the bread and the wine, does
therein deliver to them the covenant of grace sealed to
assure them of the truth and certainty thereof. This is a
sign between Him and them that they accept His
gospel treasures upon gospel terms. He will be their
God, will bestow on them every needful blessing, and
will come and make His abode with them.

As the Lord seals His part, so His people set their
seal to their part of the covenant. As the covenant is
mutual, so is the sealing. God's giving is His sealing,
and their receiving is theirs; their receiving the elements from the hand of the Lord, their eating and
drinking, is their seal to witness their acceptance of

God on His own terms. There is not a man that thus accepts and sets to His seal to whom the seal of God does not stand good. He has it under the very hand and seal of God that he is pardoned; that grace and peace, and, with these, strength to wage war against the world, the flesh, and the devil shall be imparted to him, together with all things necessary unto life and salvation.

The covenant of God encourages His people on in their warfare; it assures not only a crown to the conqueror but assistance and strength to the combatant. God will be not only the Rewarder but the Helper of all those who seek Him. He has said, "I will never leave thee, nor forsake thee," Hebrews 13:5. Hereupon, you may boldly say, "The Lord is my Helper." He has said, "Then will I sprinkle clean water upon you, and ye shall be clean: from all your filthiness, and from all your idols, will I cleanse you. A new heart also will I give you, and a new spirit will I put within you: and I will take away the stony heart out of your flesh, and I will give you a heart of flesh. And I will put My Spirit within you, and cause you to walk in My statutes, and ye shall keep My judgments, and do them. And ye shall dwell in the land that I gave to your fathers; and ye shall be My people, and I will be your God," Ezekiel 36:25-28.

What cannot the Spirit of the Lord do? The old heart and the world are close friends, but God will take away this old heart and will give to His people another, even a new heart.

Trust in God; set to your seal that God is true, and then you may say with the Psalmist, "Whom have I in heaven but Thee? And there is none upon earth that I

desire beside Thee. My flesh and my heart faileth, but
God is the strength of my heart, and my portion for
ever," Psalm 73:25-26. And again, "The Lord is my light
and my salvation; whom shall I fear? The Lord is the
strength of my life; of whom shall I be afraid? When
the wicked, even mine enemies and my foes, came
upon me to eat up my flesh, they stumbled and fell.
Though a host should encamp against me, my heart
shall not fear; though war should rise against me, in
this will I be confident. One thing have I desired of the
Lord, that will I seek after; that I may dwell in the
house of the Lord all the days of my life, to behold the
beauty of the Lord and to inquire in His temple. For in
the time of trouble He shall hide me in His pavilion; in
the secret of His tabernacle shall He hide me; He shall
set me upon a rock. And now shall mine head be lifted
up above mine enemies round about me: therefore will
I offer in His tabernacle sacrifices of joy; I will sing, yea,
I will sing praises unto the Lord," Psalm 27:1-6.

If you have engaged yourselves to be the servants of
the Lord, you must no longer be servants of the world;
you cannot serve two masters. Then, your renouncing
the world is necessarily included in your covenant
obligation.

Dear Christian friends, we would advise you, as often as you come before the Lord in this ordinance, to
use such words as these: "O my God and Father, I am
sensible of the plague of my earthly heart and the
tyranny of these worldly lusts; how impetuously they set
upon me, how imperiously they lead me on after them,
how false and unfaithful they have made me to my
God, how ordinarily I am led away by them against my
covenant and my conscience. But I here bewail it. It is

my grief and my shame that ever I have been so false
and unworthy. Behold now again, in Thy fear, I open
my mouth to the Lord. I take hold of Thy Word and I
hang upon Thy help; let the Lord, my Righteousness,
be my strength. In His name, I again lift my hand to
the Most High, solemnly attesting before Thee, the
Lord, that I so avow Thee to be my God and so entirely
and unreservedly make over myself unto Thee that,
through Thy grace within me, I will henceforth, while I
live, be the resolved enemy of the world, and that I
will, in Thy strength, use all Thy means for the over-
coming of it. I will study; I will watch; I will pray
against, restrain, and resist all the motions and temptations by which I have been so often led aside and overcome. I give myself, my money, my strength, my facul-
ties, my time—all that I have—unto the Lord. Lord,
take me at my word and all that I have for Thy service.
I am Thine, save me. Thou, who know all things, know
that I would not lie unto Thee, but that I sincerely in-
tend, in Thy strength, to stand to this word. In testimony whereof, I here take this holy Sacrament from
Thine hands. I have opened my mouth unto Thee, the
Lord; help me, and I will not go back."

Oh, friends, were there this solemn and express
transaction between your souls and God at every pe-
riod when you partake of the Lord's Supper, and if you
thus lived in the consciousness of this obligation, and
in the dread of being found false to God, what might it
not lead to! What a wound might be given to the head
of the deadly enemy!

In the sacrament of the Lord's Supper, the blessings of the new testament are exhibited. Your partak-
ing of it may be regarded as your coming into the gar-

den of your Lord to eat His pleasant fruits.

It is written, "I sat down under his shadow with great delight, and his fruit was sweet to my taste," Song of Solomon 2:3. These fruits of the Spirit of Christ are "love, joy, peace, longsuffering, gentleness, goodness, faith, meekness, temperance," Galatians 5:22-23. It is through, and by virtue of, the righteousness of Christ alone that any redeemed sinner can take of these delightful fruits.

Our blessed Lord Jesus Christ is called "THE LORD OUR RIGHTEOUSNESS," Jeremiah 23:6. He shall convince the world of righteousness, that is, of His righteousness. He shall make manifest to the world, which lies in wickedness, that in Him there is righteousness and that He has, in the name and on the behalf of those who believe on Him, fulfilled all righteousness. Thereby, He has a treasure of righteousness to bestow and, wherewith, to clothe all those who come unto God by Him, to whom He is made wisdom, righteousness, sanctification, and redemption, 1 Corinthians 1:30. Righteousness of your own, you have none; but, behold, here is righteousness for you.

The fruits of the Spirit of Christ are sweet, and the thoughts of Christ are precious. His words are sweet, "sweeter than honey and the honeycomb," Psalm 19:10. His house and His dwelling is sweet. "How amiable are Thy tabernacles, O Lord of Hosts!" Psalm 84:1. To those who believe, Christ is precious, 1 Peter 2:7.

Ask the guilty if redemption is not sweet, if pardon is not sweet. Ask the prisoner if liberty is not sweet. Ask the debtor if the blotting out of his debts is not sweet. Ask those who labor under the pangs of a guilty conscience if peace of conscience is not sweet. Ask those who feel the sentence of death within themselves if the assurance of the love of God is not sweet. If you know what blood-guiltiness means, you will find precious sweetness in the blood of atonement.

How sweet are the fruits of the Spirit! Is not love sweet? Is not holy joy sweet? Is not godly sorrow sweet? The mournings and meltings for sin have infinitely more sweetness in them than the joys and mirth of sinners.

Ask those who walk in the light of the Lord and have tasted that the Lord is gracious what they would take in exchange for those comforts wherewith they feel themselves comforted of God.

Are you resolved, by the grace of God, while you live, never to turn back and give over your following of Christ nor to sit down by anything short of an universal conformity to His image and will?

Are you crucified with Christ? Is the world crucified to you, and you to the world? Is the old man slain within you? Feel all the limbs of the old man and see if there is not life still found in some of them. Feel the heart of the old man; are not self-will, self-love, and the love of the world yet alive? Are not bitterness and wrath, envy and malice, alive in him? Examine the head of the old man; are not pride and self-conceit lodged there? Observe the eyes, the ears, the tongue, and the way; does not the old man live in these? Are not the eyes pleased with beholding vanity and the ears itching after lies and deceits? Is not the sound of him upon the tongue, and the show of him in the countenance, habit, and whole way of life? Feel the pulses of the old man, mark his breathings and pantings; are they not after earth still?

But happy and blessed will it be for you if, after a strict search, you find that you have put off the old man, with his deeds, which is corrupt according to the deceitful lusts and have put on the new man which, after God, is created in righteousness and true holiness. Then you will have evidence that you are the disciples of Christ, in the witness of the Holy Spirit with your spirit that you are His indeed.

The precious fruits of the Spirit of Christ, thus exhibited in the Sacrament of the Lord's Supper, will give you the means to gain advantages against the world. Every soul has its cravings, and these must be supplied either by the Spirit of God or by the world. He who has not the Spirit of God, here is a man for the world; he who is empty of the world, here is a soul for God. He who is taken up with the pleasures of sin will despise the joys of religion; he who is delighted with the pleasures of religion will slight the joys of the world.

The precious fruits of the Spirit of Christ are the means of renewing the strength of saints. This staff of bread will be the strength of their hearts. They are the weak souls whom the world conquers.

The Lord Jesus Christ gives the best gifts to His people. The gifts of Christ enlarge the heart and expand the soul of a believer to take in more of Himself. Though believers are but a little flock, though they are but a remnant, though they are but a fountain sealed, a spring shut up, a garden enclosed—yet Christ looks for that from them which the world will not render to Him. He looks for that love from them; He expects that service from them, that honor from them, that godly fear from them, and those prayers and praises from them which the world refuses to render to Him. "A son honoreth his father, and a servant his master; if then I be a Father, where is Mine honor? And if I be a Master, where is My fear?" Malachi 1:6.

As God, then, gives to His people the best gifts, should they not trust and depend upon Him for lesser gifts? Does God give you a crown, and will you not trust Him for bread? Does He give you a kingdom, and will you not trust Him for a cottage? Has He given you Himself, His Son, His Spirit, and His grace, and will you not trust Him to give you bread, raiment, health, strength, friends, and all other necessary mercies? Will you trust that man for much who has given you but a little, and will you not trust God for a little who has given you so much? "He that spared not His own Son, but delivered Him up for us all, how shall He not with Him also freely give us all things?" Romans 8:32.

Victory consists in looking to the reward.

There is a glorious reward for all the noble soldiers of Christ set before them in the gospel. These are the words of our gracious Lord: "To him that overcometh will I give to eat of the hidden manna, and will give him a white stone, and in the stone a new name written, which no man knoweth saving he that receiveth it," Revelation 2:17. Again, "To him that overcometh will I grant to sit with Me in My throne, even as I also overcame, and am set down with My Father in His throne," Revelation 3:21. Here is the reward of victorious saints: the hidden manna, the white stone, the new name, and the throne. What an encouragement it is to the heart to have the reward in full view!

It was said concerning our Lord, "Who for the joy that was set before Him endured the cross, despising the shame, and is set down at the right hand of the throne of God," Hebrews 12:2. Then, "Let us run with patience the race that is set before us, looking unto Jesus, the Author and Finisher of our faith." Let us run, looking to Jesus; let us hear, looking to Jesus; let us watch, let us wrestle, let us contend against the world, the flesh, and the devil, looking to Jesus. The cross is here presented to us; and, in the cross, the throne. If we suffer with Christ, we shall reign with Him, we shall be glorified with Him.

Lift up the hands that hang down, and confirm the feeble knees. Behold the Captain of your salvation whose reward is with Him and whose work is before Him. Do you say that it is hard to follow Christ and that it is hard to forsake all for Christ? Can you now say so, when He shows you the treasure He has for His followers? Open your eyes, look upon that treasure, and then see if all the labors, losses, and sufferings of this life are worthy to be compared to that glory which shall be revealed.

Victory consists in being good stewards.

Receive all the good things of the world as talents, for which you must give an account. Consider yourselves as stewards of all that you have. You have nothing but what is your Master's and for which you must be responsible to Him. You may as well reckon yourselves to be your own makers as your own masters; and you may as well reckon yourselves to be your own masters as to be unaccountable for what you have.

If you have riches and estates, if you have friends, if you have honors and dignities, if you have a large proportion of bodily health and good endowments of mind, you have so much the more to reckon for. The more you have committed to your trust, the more you will have to account for. If the sentence for hiding one talent in the earth was thus dreadful, "Cast ye the unprofitable servant into outer darkness: there shall be weeping and gnashing of teeth," Matthew 25:30, what will your judgment be if you misspend your five talents?

Your covetous heart may say, "Here is an opportunity for you to be rich," but work as hard as you will, get as much as ever you can, and know that whatever you have gotten is none of yours. You should earn so that you may have so much more to use for God. Not a house, not a field, not one penny of all that you have labored for, should be expended but for God.

Your slothful heart may say, "Here is ease, here is rest for you"' but know that you must be answerable for your leisure and your time as well as for every other talent. This earth will never constitute a rest or home. The Christian, while on earth, must be on his journey and pilgrimage; ever busy, ever active.

Your ambitious heart may say, "Here is fame for you, here are honors, here is the love, good will, and good opinion of men for you"; but know that, on this very account, you are called to labor more seriously and diligently for the Lord. These are the heavenly Master's goods, which He gives to you to use for His service. Have you wealth? Look to it, for God will look for it. Then, honor the Lord with your substance. Have you dignities, and are you set in authority? Take heed and see to it that you are faithful in your office; woe to you if you neglect the charge of the Lord. Have you the love and good will of men? This gives you the fairer opportunity, and thereby imposes on you the greater necessity to deal plainly with them in counseling, admonishing, and reproving them, as occasion shall require. You owe them much service and you shall pay dearly for the neglect of it.

Your voluptuous heart may say, "Here are pleasures for you; here are fine clothes, gaieties, and pastimes; here are large mansions, gardens and fields, and pleasant meats and drinks." But what will you do with them? You may take what will be useful and serviceable to the ends of your being to glorify your God, but take no more at your utmost peril.

The more you have of this world, the more you will be put to the hard duty of self-denial. You must crucify your flesh the more by how much the more you have to satisfy it. Whatever you have before you and however much you covet after it, you must not touch more than your allowance.

Then let each one reason thus: "Why should I so eagerly wish for more than I have? Have I not trouble enough already, labor and care enough already? Have I not enough to answer for already? It is so hard to be faithful in a little, how then shall I do if I am ruler over much? It is so hard to deny my flesh when I have nothing to satisfy it, how shall I refuse it when it lusts for what I have in my hand?"

Say to your heart, "Away with that load, though of gold or greatness, which is more than I can bear without the neglect of God or my soul. Let me be entrusted with nothing but what I am able to steward well; and whatever I have, let me be so faithful that I may give up my account with joy and not with grief, which would be unprofitable for me."

If you could but see talent written upon every worldly comfort and a rendering back to God to be the motto upon every talent, your flesh would be suffered to make but short meals on what you have and would be less greedy after a larger allowance.

What is it that makes prosperity so pleasant to earthly minds? "Oh, here is a feast for my flesh. Eat, drink, and be merry; here is enough for many years. Appetite, take your fill; here is a full table before you. Pride, spare not for charges; put on your attire; deck yourself with ornaments; crown yourself with garlands; fear not, you shall not want enough to maintain you. Soul, take your pleasure; arise, choose what will delight you; withhold not yourself from any joy. The sun shines upon your tabernacle, put away sorrow from you. See the store you have about you, varieties of all that you love; go feed yourself on whatever you like best; squeeze out the juice of all your fruits; fill your cup and be merry." Similar to this is the language of the poor sensualist.

It is no wonder that men hunger after this world who know no better feeding. But those who have eaten of the hidden manna should not lust after quails. Those whom God has fed in His green pastures and those whom God has led by His still waters should not live in the sandy plains or stubble-fields of the world. Those whose souls God has made well-watered gardens will not thirst after the putrid pools of the wilderness.

The proud and voluptuous, the greedy horse-leeches, the oppressing extortioners, the riotous livers, the proud profligates, those sons of Belial whose life is nothing else but a raking together of fuel to maintain their fires dancing before them and sacrificing all their virtue, modesty, yea, and humanity in those flames, may well tremble in the prospect of the great Day of Judgment. If these most brutish among the people would but view the reckoning they have to make of their Master's goods, all hoarded up in the dark or spent in the broad daylight of their shame, and consider how this account will pass in the Judgment, this might rust out the comfort of all their treasures, stain the beauty of all their pleasant ways, and cool their eager desiring after them.

He who falls into the hands of his riches, falls into the hands of his foolish and hurtful lusts. He who falls into the hands of these, falls into the hands of the devil, into temptation and snares; and he who falls into temptation is swimming down the stream into perdition and destruction. "They that will be rich fall into temptation and a snare, and into many foolish and hurtful lusts, which drown men in destruction and perdition," 1 Timothy 6:9.

He who dreads not temptation knows not himself. Do you know what weak and silly things you are; how ignorant of Satan's devices you are; what poor, weak, and wavering hearts you have, apt to be led away with every lust and apt to take fire from every spark? The devil watches and, yet, do you sleep? If you know not your own weakness, if you are not sensible how hard it is for you to resist and how easily you are overcome by temptation, you are strangers to yourselves. Have you had no sad experiences of your broken peace, of your wounded spirits, and of your wasted consciences to remind you how you have come off with loss? Then, stir up yourselves to resist temptations but recollect that no grace acts until faith sets it to work. Alas! There is not one of us who has not too often proved our own utter weakness.

Consider, friends, it may be that you are of a covetous heart and an earthly mind. You perhaps bewail and abhor yourselves for it. You confess it to God, pray against it, covenant against it; and perhaps you may have gotten your hearts a little raised to things above. You can scorn this earth and hope that you shall never be so taken with these beggarly things again; and yet, no sooner has the devil gotten you abroad, or into your houses among your treasures, or into your fields among your sheep and oxen, but your hearts are gone presently after them. All prayers and tears and vows are forgotten, and you are as busy and eager after the world as ever.

Perhaps you are possessed of a vain and frothy spirit, given to vanity, sensual mirth and pleasures; and, when you come to pray or humble yourselves, when you are alone and have freedom to be conversant about the matters of your souls, you may, for a time, become a little serious. With the sense of eternity falling upon you, with your souls taking a walk to the grave and looking over to those deeps that are on the other side, your spirits may be perhaps steadied and put into a more sober frame. You hope that you shall never evaporate into such froth and folly again; and yet, behold, as soon as you fall into company with vain persons and have been entertained awhile with their unholy merriments, you soon become as one of them.

It may be that you are of a peevish and froward spirit, and this has cost you dearly with many tears and troubles of heart. Sometimes, perhaps, you have prayed and found yourselves humbled into more meekness, patience, and quietness of spirit. Yet the next cross that came, if but a very look, a disrespectful word, nay, maybe but a surmise or a jealousy of a slighting thought, has put you beside all your patience and set you all in a flame.

How many such experiences have you had of yourselves? Have you not often found it thus? Must you not acknowledge it has been thus again and again? Have not these been sometimes your wishes, at such times, when you have felt yourselves in a better frame: "Oh, that it might be ever thus! Oh, that this might hold, that I might never sink into this earthliness or swell with this vanity or anger again! Oh, this slippery and unstable heart! I fear it. I doubt how it will serve me. If the world or this flesh calls me away or if any temptation comes, either to entice me or to cross me, all this calm and serenity will, I fear, become clouds and tempests. Speak, Christian! Has it not been thus many a time? Oh, what a weak thing are you!"

Dear friends, study thoroughly the evils of temptation and be convinced that the prosperities of the world are most active temptations. Receive them as such and then see if this will not cool your love for the world.

How dreadful will it be for you to be found faithless to God in the Judgment Day. It is not who shall stand in the synagogue or sit in the palace but who shall stand in the judgment. It is not who has been clothed in purple, fared sumptuously, lived deliciously; it is not who has obtained the fairest house, the largest estate, the highest honors; but it is who has been the faithful steward of his Lord's gifts! This will be the concerning question in this great and solemnly awful day.

What if this should be your case, to be brought down from your high places, to be thrust out of your mansions, to be snatched out of your shops or your fields, to be arrested at your tables in the midst of the feast and carried away before your Judge, with the account of unprofitable servants or unfaithful stewards. Oh, how dreadful will be your appearance at that day! Where will you hide yourselves? How will you bear the frown of the Lord Jesus Christ, before whom your own consciences shall arraign and accuse you as faithless, false, and wicked servants?

> Oh! that fire, before whose face
> Heaven and earth shall find no place:
> Oh, those eyes! whose angry light
> Must be the day of that dread night.
>
> Oh, that trump! whose blast shall run
> An even round with the circling sun,
> And from the murmuring graves shall bring
> The risen dead to meet their King.
>
> Oh, that book! whose leaves so true
> Will set the world in judgment due:
> Oh, that Judge! whose hand, whose eye
> None can endure; yet none can fly.
>
> Mercy, O Lord! mercy I cry,
> With blushing cheek and streaming eye;
> Great though my sin, love can forgive;
> Oh, may my soul through Jesus live!

Those mercies, Lord, thy saints have found,
Who've been by Him confess'd and crown'd,
Hope tells my heart the same may be
Through Him obtained, and that by me.

Though both my prayers and tears combine,
Both worthless are, for they are mine.
But Thou thy bounteous self still be;
And show Thou art, by saving me.

Were these things duly weighed, there would not
be such striving after the world nor such mourning
under its wants. He who had least would not murmur
at his poverty, and he who had most would not boast of
his riches. He who had least would be content, and he
who had most would be afraid; and all would conclude
that abundance is less to be desired and want less to be
feared.

Think daily more and more of God and of the everlasting kingdom. Think on the way that leads to
heaven, on the dangers that lie in the way, on the
dread of perishing in the way, on the beauty, pleasure,
and comfort of being upright in the way, and on the
reward and prize that are at the end of the way.

Be thinking of heaven and heavenly things; and, if
you will be thinking of earth too, think of the dark
places of the earth and the dark side of its brightness.
Think of the precipices, the marshes, the quicksands,
the barren mountains and desolate wildernesses, the
briars, the thorns, and the wild beasts of the earth. Our
meaning is, if you will study the world, study its vanity,
vexations, and the danger you are in of being lost or
swallowed up by it.

Dear friends, there is a day of mercy, but there is

also a day of despair. However satisfied you may be with yourselves now, a day may yet come when this awful confession may be forced from you: "Lord, I am he who slighted Thee. I set at nought Thy counsels, despised Thy covenant, trampled upon Thy blood, and preferred my goods, my pleasures, and my lusts before Thy love. I am he who, when Thou called, would not come; whom Thou with kindness invited, but I would not come. When Thou offered pardon and healing, I cared not for pardon and also refused to be healed. I chose this world for my portion. I have loved it and served it. When I should have been praying or listening, minding my soul, and laying up treasure in heaven, I was busy in following my worldly affairs, looking to my earthly happiness, and neglecting all Thy love, mercy, and kindness."

Seek, by the grace of God, to hold your affections under government. "He that . . . ruleth his spirit is better than he that taketh a city," Proverbs 16:32, and no wonder, for he has taken the whole world captive.

Our affections are blind guides, and where will the blind lead us? If we lived by faith, we should get up out of this earthly country. We should then come to know that God is infinitely better than creatures and that following creatures is forsaking God.

Directions for holding the affections right.

For the better holding of your affections right, take these two directions:

1. Seek to "Keep yourselves in the love of God, looking for the mercy of our Lord Jesus Christ unto eternal life," Jude 21. Seek the grace of God that you

may be able to keep up a right understanding of God; this will keep up your affections to Him and will keep them off from the world. But if the heart is not set upon God, its affections will be surely set on the world. Stand fast in the love of God in order that you may not be carried away by the love of the world.

2. Whatever you love in the world, let it be also your fear. Nothing has more advantage over us, to steal away our hearts from God, than the things of the world which we love; whatever you love in all the world, be it a relation whom you love, be it a friend or companion whom you love. Have you money, a pleasant habitation, gardens, orchards, fields, or farms that you are delighted with? Oh, be jealous of them and keep your distance from them! Say, "You come for my soul, O my relations, my friends, my lands, my house, my money. I must be upon my guard against you for you come to steal away my heart."

If what you love is not also your fear, it is likely to be your loss and sorrow. Children who have been over-loved often repay their parents' doting by becoming thorns in their sides and barbed arrows in their hearts. Whatever you overlove, you may expect to find your cross or your curse. What will your friends or your money be when either you have lost them or your souls by them?

What is it that lies in the way of the gospel, that obstructs its course and hinders its work upon souls? Why, is it that Christ is not more gladly and generally received? Oh, this is that which hinders; it would deprive men of many a sweet morsel and many a pleasant draft! It would pull off their vain habits and luxurious fashions. It would cut off their worldly pleasures. No more indulging their appetites; no more pleasing their eyes, ears, and palates, if the Lord Jesus Christ was once welcomed by the heart. Now men can take their liberty to make provision for the flesh, even to excess. They can feed themselves with the finest, clothe themselves with the best, and wallow in all sorts of sensualities. They can fetch in load upon load, they can dig in every mine, and they can plow and reap in every field that the world has. Now none but Christ can hinder them.

If they once give ear to Him, that will mar all sensuality and covetousness. Then, they must keep within bounds and neither get nor spend more than He allows them. They must keep to their allowance, and that but a short allowance such as will be too strait for corrupt flesh and blood to submit to.

How plain it is that men's eyes and ears, which are so open to the world and its vanities, do, as it were, invite and call in all the help the world can give to resist Christ and His work. They call in all the baits and temptations that the whole world is furnished with to divert and turn aside the heart from hearkening to Christ.

Make a solemn surrender of yourselves and all you have to the government and disposal of God. Lay down all at His feet, and resolve to take up nothing but with His leave and for His use.

Let the Lord have the whole ordering of you in body, soul, and spirit. Say to the Lord, but say it in godly sincerity and truth, "Here we offer and present unto Thee ourselves, our souls and bodies, to be a reasonable, holy, and lively sacrifice unto Thee." Alas, how many thousands of times have multitudes used these

very words with their lips, while their lives and actions
have proved that these words have but made up the
language of the hypocrite?

Seek no other things nor any greater abundance of
them than God allows you to seek. Buy not a house,
nor field, nor food, nor merchandise but as God allows
you. Go not into the fair, or the market, or the shop,
or over the seas but as God sends you. Drive not that
trade or that bargain concerning which you cannot say,
"I am herein trading for God." Humbly submit to the
Lord, that He may appoint for you your work, your
rest, your labor and your profit; be content with what
He gives. Seek not great things for yourselves, and
quarrel not with the providence of God if, by all your
seeking, you get nothing.

Seek no more, nor no other things than God would
have you, and seek them no other way than in the way
and order which He appoints. God has other works
than these for you to do. God has other things than
these for you to seek. God says, "Seek ye My face."
Then say, "Thy face, Lord, will I seek." Have you grace?
Have you peace? Have you enough of these? Is there
no more now to be done, no more to be gotten? Are
there not ways between you and glory that need your
care how to get over? Have your souls no enemies left
alive? Are your lusts dead, the world vanquished, and
the devil trodden underfoot? Have you as much grace
as you need; as much faith, love, and patience as you
need? Have you no need of that prayer, "Lord, increase our faith"? Are you past these counsels: "Grow
in grace, and in the knowledge of our Lord and Savior
Jesus Christ," 2 Peter 3:18; or "Hold that fast which
thou hast," Revelation 3:11? Or is there not rather

much of this work to be done which God would first have be done?

Yea, with some of you, is it not all too late? No interest for your souls, no knowledge, no grace obtained; nothing of the work of conversion, nothing of the work of repentance existing? The first stone of the new building is yet to be laid, yea, not so much as the old rubbish removed, not an evil affection cast out, your worldly hopes not yet extinguished, your hard hearts not so much as touched?

What! Is there nothing cared for the other world by so many of you, and are you yet so busy for this world? This is not as God would have it. Go then and ask counsel of God, saying, "Lord, what wilt Thou have me to do?"

Keep and lay up no more by you than God would have you. Say of all that you lay up, "This is the property of God and does not belong to me." Let no stolen goods be found with you; all is stolen, stolen into your purses and stolen into your houses, which the Lord would have otherwise disposed of. Be not then laying up when God calls you to lay out. Be not then sparing when God would have you to be expending.

It is written, "For ye know the grace of our Lord Jesus Christ, that, though He was rich, yet for your sakes He became poor, that ye through His poverty might be rich," 2 Corinthians 8:9.

You have, in these words, an urgent call upon you to give up all you are and all you have to Christ.

Our blessed Lord was born in poor circumstances and lived a life of poverty that you, thereby, might be made rich—rich in the love and favor of God, rich in the blessings and promises of the new covenant, rich in the hope of eternal life, and rich in every Christian grace and work. This is a good reason why you should abound in every work of mercy, liberality, and love towards all around you, thus adorning the gospel of the Lord and Savior and, moreover, because you live upon the charity of the Lord Jesus Christ.

God says to the worldly rich men, "Your riches are corrupted, your garments are moth-eaten, your gold and silver is cankered, and the rust of them shall be a witness against you and shall eat your flesh as if it were fire. You have heaped treasure together for the last days," James 5:2-4. See, here is treasure for the moth, the canker, and the rust. Oh, let there be no more such heaping up, no more such treasuring up for hell!

Lay down all you have at the feet of God; neither seek nor use anything but according to His order and will. Never let self set you to work; leave nothing to its disposal; feed not your eye or your appetite; feed not your pride or your covetousness. When worldly lusts are dead and the temptations of the world are conquered, the world which was your lord will, henceforth, become your servant.

You may be affrighted and daunted in view of the hardships you may have to suffer in contending against the world, but try the narrow way and seek by faith in God (who, as He is the Shield and Rock, so is He the strength of His people) to overcome it. Then, you may find yourselves to be another sort of men, and you may be led to confess that it is better to be a doorkeeper in the house of God than to dwell in the tents of wickedness.

Be acquainted with this way, and you will be acquainted with God. Your joys will be spiritual, prevalent, and lasting. You will have comfort in life and comfort in death. When you have neither wealth, nor health, nor the happiness of this world, you may yet have that comfort and peace which the world cannot give or take away. When all means are denied to you, or taken from you, yet you may have solid, real comfort. Your graces will be active and victorious. You will be as those who stand on the top of an exceeding high mountain. You look down upon the plains which lie stretched below you; how small do the fields, woods, and countries seem to you! Countries and towns seem but little spots. Thus will your souls, when justified through faith in Christ and sanctified by the Holy Spirit, look with contempt on all things here below.

The men of this world will seem to be but as grasshoppers, and the busy, contentious, covetous world but as a nest of ants. Men's threatenings will be no occasion of terror to you, nor the honors of this world a desirable happiness. Temptations will be more harmless, as having so lost their strength; afflictions less grievous, as having so lost their sting; and mercies will be better known and relished by you.

Dear friends, will you live this blessed life or not? If life is lost through your unbelief, be it known to you that you will prove the greatest losers yourselves. If you value not this heavenly life, how can you say with truth that you value heaven? And if you value it not, no wonder if you are shut out from it.

The power of godliness is found in the actings of the soul. Take heed that you stand not in a vain, deluding form. You should mind nothing but what tends to God and His glory. You are almost out of this life already. Disease or other means will shortly dismiss your souls. The worms wait to feed upon your bodies. What if your pulse must beat a few strokes more; what if you have a few more breaths to fetch before you breathe your last; and what if you have a few more nights to sleep before you sleep in the dust? Alas! What will this be when all is gone, and is it not almost gone already?

Verily, shortly you will see your glass just run out, and each may say, "My life is nearly gone; my time is nearly gone; it is past recalling. There is nothing now but heaven or hell before me. Oh, where then should my heart be now but in heaven!"

It is a dreadful matter for a man to have strange and doubtful thoughts of heaven when he lies dying. What other thoughts but strange can a man have who never thought seriously of heaven till then? Strangeness naturally excites fear as familiarity does delight. What else makes a wild beast flee from man when domestic animals take pleasure in his company? So will you flee from God, if this strangeness is not removed. Is it not a pity that a child should be so strange to his own father as to fear nothing more than to go into his presence and to think himself best off when he is farthest from him?

Alas! How little do many professors of religion differ from the world, either in their comforts or willingness to die, and all because they live so strange to God who is the Father of His people. Beyond a few outside duties, or talking of controversies and doctrines of religion, or forbearing the practice of particular sins, how little do too many of those who profess strict religion differ from other men, when God has prepared so vast a difference hereafter. If a word concerning God falls in now and then in their conversation, alas, how slight is it, how superficial and heartless!

Victory consists in heavenly joys.

Oh, what a life might men live if they were but willing and diligent! God would have their joys to be far more than their sorrows. He would have them to have no sorrow but what tends to joy, and no more sorrow than their sins have made necessary for their good. How much do those persons wrong God and themselves who either make their thoughts of God the inlet of their sorrows or let these offered joys lie by as neglected or forgotten? Many there are who think that it is not worth much time and trouble to seek God and the joys at His right hand. But as these men obey not the commands of God, which require them to have their conversation in heaven and to set their affections on things above, so they willfully make their own lives miserable by refusing the joys that God has set before them. See what abundance of other mischiefs follow the lack of these heavenly joys.

1. The lack of these heavenly joys will dampen, if not destroy, love to God. According as men apprehend the bounty and exceeding love of God and His purpose to make them eternally happy, so much will it raise their love. Love to God and delight in Him are still conjoined.

2. This lack will cause men to have infrequent and unpleasant thoughts of God, for their thoughts will follow that course in which they delight. Did they more delight in God than in the world, their thoughts would run as freely after Him as they now run from Him.

3. This lack will cause men to use an infrequent
and unpleasant speech concerning God; for who will
care for speaking of one for whom he feels no regard?
What makes men still talk of worldliness or wickedness,
but that this is more pleasant to them than talking of
God.

4. This lack will deprive man of all desire to serve
God, because they have no delight in Him or any sweet
thoughts of heaven. It is no wonder that men complain
that they are backward in duty, that they have no delight in prayer, in Sacraments, or in reading the Word
of God. If they once delighted in God, they would easily delight in duty, especially that which brings them
into the nearest converse with Him; but, till then, no
wonder they are weary of all. Does not this cause many
persons to go on so heavily in secret duties, like the ox
in the furrow that will go no longer than he is driven
and is glad when he is unyoked?

5. This lack threatens to pervert men's judgments
concerning the ways of God, because they have no
delight in looking to God. The soul will not much care
for that truth which is not accompanied with suitable
goodness, and it will more easily be drawn to believe
that to be false which it does not delightfully apprehend to be good; which, doubtless, is no small
cause of the prejudice which ungodly men and formal-
ists have against the ways of God. Affection holds its object faster than bare judgment. Had men a true delight
in God and heavenly things, it would rectify their
judgments better than all the arguments in the world.
Those who do not have this delight will quarrel with
the ordinances and ways of God.

6. It is the lack of this heavenly joy in God that

causes men to entertain the delights of the flesh. This is the true cause of men's voluptuousness and flesh-pleasing. The soul will not rest without some kind of delight. If it has nothing to delight in, either in hand or in hope, it will vex itself with sorrow and despair. Men must have their sweet cups, or delicious fare, or fine apparel, or drunkenness, or revelings, or evil affections to make up a delight, while they should delight in God. How these have served instead of God will be known by the ungodly when they meet at judgment. If men were acquainted with the heavenly life, there would be no need to have laws against Sabbath-breaking and riotousness. Nor would persons need to go to an alehouse or a tavern, to the playhouse or the ballroom, for their delight or happiness. They would have a far sweeter pleasure and happiness nearer at hand.

7. This lack will leave men under the power of every affliction. They will have nothing to comfort and ease them in their sufferings but the empty, ineffectual pleasures of the world; and when these are gone, where then is their delight?

8. his lack will make men unwilling to die, for who would wish to go to God when he does not delight in Him? Who would want to leave his pleasures here except for greater happiness? Oh, if the people of God would learn more of this heavenly life and take up their delight in God more while they live, they would not tremble and be disconsolate at the tidings of death!

9. Yea, this lack will lay men open to the power of every temptation. A little thing will entice a man from that which he has no pleasure in.

10. Last, this lack of heavenly joy is a dangerous preparative to total apostasy. A man will hardly keep on for long in a way that he has no delight in, nor use the means if he has no delight in the end. He is as a beast which, if you drive him in a way that he does not like to go, will be turning in to every gap. If men are religious only in form and appear religious only in their outward conduct, not in the sincerity of their hearts, they will shortly be overcome if temptations are strong.

How many young people have we known who, by good education, or the persuasion of friends, or through fear of hell, have kept up prayers, sermons, and religious society for awhile like birds in a cage, when they would rather have been indulging themselves in pleasures or dissipation; and, at last, they have broken loose when restraint has been taken off and have forsaken the way that they never took pleasure in? You may see, then, that it is not a matter of indifference whether you entertain this heavenly joy or not; nor is the loss of your present comfort all the inconvenience that follows the neglect of seeking heavenly delights.

And now, dear friends, we have tried to lay before you a precious, heavenly employment. Would you but pursue it, it would make you happy indeed. To delight in God is the work of angels, and the contrary is the work of devils. Make conscience of this duty and rely upon God for the blessed influence of His Spirit, and then you will not wish to change situations with any of the ungodly, even the chiefest upon earth. But if we may judge your hearts by the backwardness of our own, we may find it hard to persuade you. What say you? Do you resolve on this heavenly course or not? Will you let go of your sinful pleasures, your worldly delights, and careful seekings after the world and daily seek after these higher joys? Let your families perceive, let your neighbors perceive, let your consciences perceive, that you are men who have your daily conversation in heaven. God has now offered to be your portion. Your neglect is your refusal. What! Refuse delights, and such delights? Take heed what you do; refuse these, you refuse all. God is willing that you should daily walk with Him and receive consolation from His Spirit.

O Thou Almighty Savior, whose goodness and mercy abound to us, Thy poor creatures, draw up these earthly hearts of ours unto Thyself and spiritualize and refine them by the influences of Thy Holy Spirit! Oh, suffer not the souls of Thy most unworthy servants to be strangers to those joys which Thou dost unfold to Thy people, or to be seldom in that way which Thou hast pointed out! But keep us, while we tarry on this earth, in daily serious breathings after Thee and in a believing, affectionate walking with Thee. And when Thou comest, oh, let us be found so doing, not hiding our talent, nor serving our lusts, nor yet asleep with our lamps unfurnished, but waiting and longing for Thy return!

Nothing less than victory will do.

Dear Christian friends, can victory over the world be bought too dearly? There is nothing in this world but what can be paid too highly for. An army may be so weakened in the fight that victory will not repair it. Crowns and kingdoms may be bought too dearly; all the royalties and revenues of the world may be pur-

chased at such a rate that they may not be a saving bargain. But can redemption from the world be paid too
highly for? Will not the salvation of the soul overpay all
charges? "What shall it profit a man, if he shall gain the
whole world, and lose his own soul?" Mark 8:36.

It is true that your being rescued from this enemy
may not be without much loss. When you conquer this
enemy, you will lose a false friend. In your conquering,
you will purchase enmity. The world will hate you. You
will not only create enemies by your conquest, but
wants, straits, labors, and cares. When you cease to be
servants to the world, think not to have an easy, idle
life. You will have more and more work to do than
ever—pursuing your enemy so that he will not rally
again upon you, watching your hearts, guarding your
eyes, governing your appetites so that they do not run
again after it, pleasing and following the Lord in all
things that He commands you. The day on which you
break off from the world and join yourselves to the
Lord, you take up a life of self-denying labor. But it is a
sweet toil. Then you must no more thirst after stolen
waters nor taste of forbidden pleasures; you must no
more walk in your former ways nor refuse the most
painful duties. Nay, not your ease only or your pleasure, but your lives, also, and all that you have must go
whenever and wherever your Lord calls you.

Nothing short of this will either obtain or secure
for you the victory. Therefore, consider whether such a
life will suit you. How will your spirits bear it when your
faint hearts shrink from it, when your proud or stub-
born hearts swell against it, when your old pleasures
and liberties, your old friends and companions, your
silver and your gold cry after you, "Can you leave us

thus? Can your souls part with us forever?"

It is hard to be a Christian. This is true in one sense, but the Christian can say, "Blessed be God, my soul is escaped, my foot is gotten out of the snare; liberty, liberty is brought to me, once a captive, and the opening of the prison to the bound. God whom I now serve, however hard His work is, is no hard Master. He gives great rewards. Were His work harder than it is, yet it is not worthy to be laid in the balance with salvation. I will not die for an easy life."

Parting words to those of this world and to the children of God.

We are now drawing to a conclusion. We will then address some parting words to those who are of this world and to those who are the children of God.

Speak, worldlings, let your consciences speak. When death comes to arrest your souls, would you choose to be found wallowing in your worldly lusts, steeped in sensuality, laden with worldly cares, loaded with earthly goods, and as empty of the knowledge and grace of God as you are this day? Would you have that written on your forehead, when you come to stand before that dreadful tribunal, which was written concerning Doeg the Edomite, "Lo, this is the man that made not God his strength; but trusted in the abundance of his riches, and strengthened himself in his wickedness"? Psalm 52:7.

Will you henceforth become enemies to the world? Will you deal with the world as an enemy; will you fear it as an enemy; will you fight against it in Christian warfare as an enemy? Shall the Lord be your God; shall the Lord be your Friend; shall the Lord be your Shield, your Refuge, and the Rock of your salvation? Will you cast away all your idols, and will you come and be reconciled to God? What say you? Will you be crucified to this world, and go on in the pilgrimage (saints are strangers and pilgrims in this world) for the other world?

God has said, "Love not the world, neither the things that are in the world," 1 John 2:15. Consider the Scripture, "Now then we are ambassadors for Christ, as though God did beseech you by us: we pray you in Christ's stead, be ye reconciled to God," 2 Corinthians 5:20.

What is the errand with which the ministers of the gospel are sent from the Lord unto you? Is it not to persuade you to be reconciled to God? The word which they preach is, therefore, called "the word of reconciliation," 2 Corinthians 5:19. Can you be reconciled to God while you hold in with the world? When they, therefore, warn you to be reconciled to God, do they not therein call you, according to the will and work of God, to be enemies to the world?

Do not both the goodness and severity of God call upon you to forsake the world and to live unto God? "Or despisest thou the riches of his goodness and forbearance and longsuffering; not knowing that the goodness of God leadeth thee to repentance?" Romans 2:4.

Do not the severities of God call you off from the world? What do the judgments of God mean, which He executes on the earth, but to drive you from broken cisterns to the fountain? What does the wormwood and the gall mean but to wean you from the ways of the world? Wherefore are your disappointments, vexations, distresses, but to tell you that this world is not your rest? What speak the winds and the storms, the floods and the fires, the sword and the famine, the thief and the moth but, "Get up, get up out of this place!" Of what use are all trials but to crucify—to crucify you to the world and to crucify the world unto you?

The Apostle, writing to the Romans, makes this earnest and affectionate appeal to them: "I beseech you therefore, brethren, by the mercies of God, that ye present your bodies a living sacrifice, holy, acceptable unto God, which is your reasonable service. And be not conformed to this world: but be ye transformed by the renewing of your mind, that ye may prove what is that good, and acceptable, and perfect will of God," Romans 12:1-2.

Worldly men mind worldly things, having their conversation in the flesh, "fulfilling the desires of the flesh and of the mind," Ephesians 2:3; but will you be conformed to them? We would take up these words and say, "We beseech you, by the mercies of God, be not conformed to this world. Will you have your conversation and take your portion with those who are strangers to Christ and to the comforts of His Spirit? We beseech you, by the mercies of God, that you do not. Do you hope for the mercy of God? Do you not live by His mercy? Has not His mercy pitied you, spared you; has not His mercy fed you and upheld you, and will you not hearken to His beseechings?"

Is not this the voice of all the kindnesses and compassions of the Lord: "Come back from your vanities, come away from following idols. Yield not yourselves any longer to the lusts of the flesh; come away. As you love mercy, come; as you have received mercy, come; as you hope for mercy, come." Is not this the voice of mercy, and shall it not prevail? Is this the rate and price you put upon the grace and mercy of God, that you will deny Him in those little things which He demands of you? What! Not a worldly pleasure to be abated, not a vain companion to be displeased, not a few handfuls of earth to be trodden underfoot for His sake?

Where is your gratitude? Is not goodness obliging? Will you show what power mercy has with you, how much you can do, how much you can give and give up for the sake of God? You, at least, who have obtained mercy, your hearts should be ready to take their flight from this wilderness to the mountains of spices.

Have your earthly minds nailed to the cross of Christ, and there will be an end to all your crosses. Then every cross that comes will, thenceforth, be so easy that it will even lose its nature.

Oh, that this might be the language of each: "Has not God given His dear Son for me? Has He not given me mercy unto life? Now take all—farms and oxen, silver and gold, honors and pleasures. Let all go, and you, O my soul, become a living sacrifice, holy and acceptable unto God. Affections, where are you? Desires, where do you run? Come back from these vanities and get up to your God. Mercy has descended, let me ascend with it and no longer dwell in the dust."

Dear friends, have you not sufficiently smarted for your folly? What is it that gives you so many rods and makes the lashes of them to cut so deep but your unmortifiedness to this world? How easy would your crosses lie, were you dead to the world!

This is the voice of the Word: "Be mortified, be crucified." Be crucified to the world or look to be crucified by the world. Let your earthly minds be nailed to the cross of Christ, and there will be an end to all your crosses.

What is there in your refusal to hearken to these calls of God? Is there anything less in it than this: "I will not be reconciled to God. I choose rather that God be my enemy than that the world be not my friend. I would rather have the wormwood and the gall than lose the milk and the honey of the world"?

Dear friends, oh, that we might hear this word from you: "We have done with all our idols. Away with them to the moles and to the bats. We have done with this vain, earthly life. No longer will we be so mad as to venture eternity for minutes, and venture the everlasting kingdom for phantoms and shadows. Come, we will hearken to the Lord this day; henceforth for the invisible world. Hitherto we have lived in pleasure; we have been written in the earth. Hitherto we have been sowing to the flesh; we have been laboring for the wind and reaping the whirlwind; we have been laying up our treasure on earth; we have been gathering in clay and throwing away manna; we have fed upon ashes and trod upon pearls. Our lives have been either a mere play or a labor for bubbles. Henceforth, for substance, for the durable riches, for the everlasting pleasures, for the bags that wax not old, for the treasure in heaven that fails not!"

But now, may there not yet be abundant hope for you? God is still gracious; still He offers pardon. For He multiplies pardons to all those who seek Him through Christ, His well-beloved Son. Go, then, take your leave of the world this day. Stay not till tomorrow, lest it again entangle you and bewitch you into another mind. This is the leave we would advise you to take; say to the world, "I am none of yours; you are none of mine. I am none of yours; I have given myself to the Lord. You are none of mine; with myself I have given away all and shall not henceforth count you any- thing. I can bear the loss of you. I can be thankful for what I enjoy and I can bear the loss of you. With what I have, I will be content; if I have not, I will be patient."

To you, faithful Christians whose hearts God has weaned from all things here below, we would say, "Value more and more this heavenly life and take your daily walk in the new Jerusalem. You seek God as your portion, and you would fain be more acquainted with your Savior; and it is your grief that your hearts are not more near to Him and that they do not more freely and passionately love and delight in Him. If you would have all this corrected and enjoy your wishes, try this life of meditation on your everlasting rest! Here is Mount Ararat where the fluctuating ark of your souls should rest. Oh, let the world see, by your heavenly lives, that religion lies in something more than opinions and disputes and a task of outward duties! Let men see in you, as imitating the life of Christ, a life they should aim at." If ever a Christian is as he ought to be, acting according to and consistent with his profession, it is when he is most serious and lively in his duty.

As Moses went up into Mount Nebo to take a survey of the land of Canaan, so the Christian ascends the mount of contemplation and takes a survey, by faith, of this rest. He looks upon the glorious, delectable mansions and can say, "Glorious things are spoken of thee, O city of God," Psalm 87:3.

Thus, as Daniel, in his captivity, three times a day, opened his window and looked towards far-off Jerusalem, when he went up to pray before the Lord, so may the believing soul, in this captivity of the body, look towards the Jerusalem which is above. And, as Paul was to the Colossians, so may he be, with regard to the glorified spirits, absent in the flesh but present in spirit, enjoying and beholding their heavenly order, Colossians 2:5.

And now, at length, here is the conqueror and this is his victory—he who has come unto God through Christ; to whom the world has ceased to be a treasure; he whose affections are set "on things above, not on things on the earth; whose life is hid with Christ in God"; he who, in all his dealings, will be true, though to his own loss; he who will be poor rather than be dishonest; he whom the whole world cannot bribe or force to be false to God; he who can use all that he has to the glory of God; he who can lack the world's good things or suffer the world's evil things; he who is happy, most happy, in being a partaker of the grace of the Lord Jesus Christ, the love of God, and the communion of the Holy Ghost; he who can deny his appetites (he is the one who really has abundance); he who is crucified with Christ; he who can lack and be content, suffer and be patient; he who is humble in the height of honor, magnanimous in the depth of danger and difficulty, he who keeps in an even, equal poise; he who is sober, temperate, and serious in all the turns and changes of his life; he who lives no longer for himself but unto Christ who died for him—he who can thus live in the world, and can die out of the world, and is willing to depart to be with Christ—he is the conqueror and here is his victory.

Go, then, and take your leave of the world; let not your hearts be satisfied until they and this world are entirely parted.

And now arise and follow after your crucified Lord. Deny yourselves, take up your cross, and follow Him, and you shall have treasure in heaven.

"Now unto Him that is able to keep you from falling, and to present you faultless before the presence of His glory with exceeding joy, to the only wise God our Savior, be glory and majesty, dominion and power, both now and ever. Amen," Jude 24-25.

Finis